THE SILENCE

THE SILENCE WE KEEP

A Nun's View of the Catholic Priest Scandal

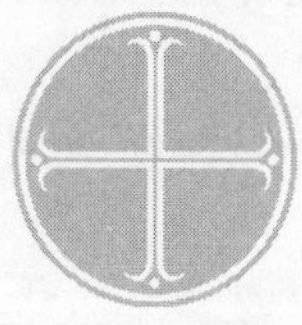

KAROL JACKOWSKI

Harmony Books / New York

Published by Harmony Books, New York, New York.
Member of the Crown Publishing Group, a division of Random House, Inc.
www.randomhouse.com

HARMONY BOOKS is a registered trademark and the Harmony Books colophon is a trademark of Random House, Inc.

Printed in the United States of America

Design by Leonard Henderson

Library of Congress Cataloging-in-Publication Data

Jackowski, Karol.
The silence we keep : a nun's view of the Catholic priest scandal / Karol Jackowski. — 1st ed.
p. cm.
1. Catholic Church — Clergy — Sexual behavior. 2. Monastic and religious life of women. 3. Catholic Church — Doctrines. I. Title.
BX1912.9.J36 2004
282 — dc21 200301161

ISBN 1-4000-5055-3

10 9 8 7 6 5 4 3 2 1

First Edition

This book is dedicated to the victims of silence.

ACKNOWLEDGMENTS

WHILE MANY OF THOSE who contributed to this book requested anonymity, there are several people whom I can acknowledge by name. From *Rosie* magazine: editorial director Rosie O'Donnell; editor-in-chief and dear friend Susan Toepfer; and executive editors Carol Kramer and Jane Farrell. Had it not been for those women, I would have kept the silence forever, at least in writing. My agent, Laurie Liss, and editors Jake Morrissey and Teryn Johnson, are the only ones I trusted as sisters with this book, along with Virginia Bell, who gave it the perfect title, as well as divine guidance and support, chapter by chapter.

Warren Mason from Saint Michael's Parish in East Longmeadow, Massachusetts, appeared like an angel out of nowhere. Having read the article in *Rosie,* Warren called to offer support, and like the research assistant every writer wished she had, he sent daily e-mail news reports from all over the country documenting priest sex scandals and cover-ups, all of which reveal the depth and breadth of the problem, without which I would have only scratched the surface. Warren Mason and Fr. Jim Scahill, pastor of Saint Michael's, are two divine voices crying out in the wilderness and in one parish where silence is so sacred that it can no longer be kept. All of the above, as well as the anonymous, wrote this book with me. And now that it's done, they're to be evermore thanked, as are you for reading this book and thinking with me about the silence we keep.

CONTENTS

A Death Blow is a Life blow to Some
Who till they died, did not alive become —
Who had they lived, had died but when
They died, Vitality begun.

EMILY DICKINSON #816

THE SILENCE WE KEEP

PREFACE

I HAD NO IDEA how much silence I had kept until I began to write this book. And had it not been for the divine coincidence of being asked to write an article on a nun's view of the Catholic priest scandal for the November 2002 issue of *Rosie* magazine, this book never would have happened. While I am a writer of books, I had no plans to work on one about the Catholic Church, much less a book that focuses on the sex crimes and cover-ups in its priesthood. News reporters and journalists are already doing an excellent job of uncovering new information almost daily, and because I don't know any pedophile priests personally, I felt that I had nothing to say. This felt like one book that just wasn't in me.

Truth be told, I didn't want to get involved in the mess we see unfolding before us now, and given the noticeable silence of sisters on the subject, I am certainly not alone. Women in the church, and nuns in particular, have been conditioned to excel in keeping personal thoughts private. Women are still believed to be incapable of rational thought and divine insight. We are still taught to silence our emotional outbursts and silly thoughts. Even in the midst of this crisis, the voice of women in the church remains wrapped in silence; perhaps they believe as I did that the matter is best left to theologians and church historians. The priesthood alone created this scandal and the responsibility of explaining how it continues to happen is theirs alone. Because only priests know the whole truth, I felt as if there was nothing for me to say. I was wrong.

Writing this book revealed all kinds of silences I was educated and trained to keep, and obviously I did find something to say. This book called me into the dark soul of the Catholic Church where I as a writer had no plans to go, but as a sister I didn't dare say no: Sisters tend to hear such calls as a call of God. As a writer and sister of forty years, I am far more drawn to write books about our spiritual lives and the ways I find to live happily ever after—books like *Ten Fun Things to Do Before You Die* (2000), and *Sister Karol's Book of Spells and Blessings* (2002). In the 1980s, I wrote fun-filled cookbooks for college students, calling them *Let the Good Times Roll* (1980) and *Home on the Range* (1982). In 1996, I published *Divine Madness,* a book about why any woman in her right mind would want to be a nun. Because nearly everyone I meet eventually wants to know the secret to my happiness, I tend to write books that reveal those secrets. I also tend to do so in an ordinary manner everyone can share—not just Catholics, and certainly not just women in the sisterhood. The secrets I find to living happily come from a God we can all know and love, and a Holy Spirit who lives and moves in all of us.

Nothing could be further removed from the happy books I've been drawn to write than the subject of sex-crimes and corruption in the Catholic priesthood, and never before have I given thought to the silence I'd kept on the subject. Never before have I been asked as I am now to say what I'm thinking. Nearly everyone I meet asks what I know about the sex scandals in the priesthood and wonder if something similar is going on in the sisterhood. All question the future of Catholicism. My response is this book: Part One talks about what I see going on in the priesthood, Part Two tells about my experiences in the sisterhood, and Part Three envisions what I see happening next.

As you read this book keep in mind that I do not speak on behalf of all nuns; nor do my views in any way represent those of the sisters in my community. What I see happening in the Catholic Church is simply one view, with additional stories from some of my sisters, nearly all of whom asked to remain anonymous. Some silences in this book are still kept. The insidious pressure to keep silent about what's happening in the Catholic Church is more real than we care to acknowledge. Most priests and sisters choose to do their work and speak their minds quietly, behind the scenes. Many who work in the church feel that breaking the silence could cost them their job and make their life miserable, even lose the support of their religious communities. Some sisters are silent because they believe priests are being falsely accused. And many, I suspect, do not see the depth of corruption that I see when we look at priesthood in the Catholic Church.

I am not alone in wondering what women think about the scandals, what we know about them, and why we remain so quiet. Given all that's happened, the voice of women remains mysteriously silent because we, too, have been victimized and abused. Women are special victims of this priesthood, as you'll find out in the pages ahead. For centuries we've been duped into submission by these "men of God," and for centuries we let ourselves be duped into believing we are not worthy of priesthood. Many women believed blindly whatever we were told, even though it made no sense and often tormented our souls. So many had faith that the voice of the priesthood was the voice of God on earth and made personal decisions accordingly—such as having more children than the body can bear and remaining faithful to abusive husbands. Many of us believed it all in silence, and many of us now suffer soulful betrayal in silence. We have been betrayed in ways we are only beginning to realize—betrayed in ways that we have never spoken of. While there may be a high personal price to be paid by those who break the silence, there's also a high personal price to be paid by those who don't.

In reading this book, you should also keep in mind that I am not a theologian or a church historian, although I've continued to educate myself in studying Catholic theology and history. Given what I've learned in my life and in my work, this book explains what I see happening in the Catholic Church today. I do, however, have good friends who are brilliant theologians, and without their help and insight, this book could not have been written. Because they, too, prefer anonymity, my hope is that this book speaks well on their behalf and on behalf of all those whose stories serve to enrich and help explain more clearly what I see going on in the priesthood.

This was not an enjoyable book to write. What's happening in the Catholic priesthood is awful and devastating enough to read in the daily news, much less to try to understand. How did we end up where we are today and what happens next? Fortunately, the news in this book does not go from bad to worse. While the look at priesthood in Part One is enough to make anyone heartsick and outraged, similar looks in Part Two on the sisterhood, and Part Three on the future of Catholicism, reveal the presence of a God far more with us than the current mess may lead us to believe. In writing this book, I rediscovered as new the sacred truths and traditions that still make me love being a Catholic. Even if you're not Catholic, there are universal truths and traditions here sacred to anyone who believes in God. My greatest hope in writing this book is that we all look seriously at the silences we keep and begin to speak to one another about what we're thinking. Keeping silent no more is the prayer on every page in this book.

PART ONE

Priesthood

Introduction

IN TRYING TO UNDERSTAND the current crisis in the Catholic priesthood, I confronted dimensions of the problem I had never noticed before. The first realization came with my seeing how much this scandal had everything to do with me. I saw how suspect the silence of the sisterhood appears now, and how these scandal-ridden times beg us to say something about what we know. I saw the voice of all women in the church as mysteriously silent, most especially my own. The second realization came as I tried to clarify the problem. I saw how accepting we've always been of some sexual relationships in the priesthood, and at the same time how outraged and betrayed we feel over the criminal abuses and cover-ups. No wonder so many feel confused soulfully. At some level, we bought into the hypocrisy.

In taking a studied look at how priesthood emerged in the Catholic Church, my heart sank when I realized how old the problem of priestly privilege and abuse is, and I still shudder every time we receive more evidence of how criminally corrupt the priesthood is. The fact that the Catholic Church survives is a daily miracle. Everything I see when I look at the Catholic priesthood led me to return to its beginning in order to understand why we are where we are today. Because the seeds of self-destruction appear to be that deeply grounded, I looked at priesthood in the early church, priesthood in the Middle Ages, and priesthood now.

In forty years as a sister, I was never asked about the priesthood. Now I am asked about it almost daily. Friend and stranger, Catholic and non, look at me as though stunned, and over and over pose the same question, "What in God's name is going on in the Catholic Church?" Most wonder what I think of the "big priest scandal" and what nuns "know about it." Both subjects top nearly every conversation I have, and both subjects called me to explain what I see happening in the Catholic Church. All of a sudden I find myself pressed to answer questions I've never been asked before and never needed to think about. All of a sudden, a scandal that had nothing to do with me became a scandal that had everything to do with me. Persistent questions called on me for answers that I didn't have, many of which still leave me speechless. The answers I did find are what make up this book.

In looking at priesthood today, it's no surprise that some attention would shift to the sisterhood and what we know. Sisters worldwide were always perceived as priests' helpers (and cheap labor). In every parish, priests were responsible for everything that happened in church, and sisters were responsible for everything that happened in school. Together they took care of what we knew as "parish life." When we looked at those who built the community life of the church, we saw priests and sisters sharing the workload, though never equally as partners. Nuns were submissive to priests, servants extraordinaire to these privileged "men of God," and major contributors to the priesthood's culture of privilege; some still are.

As young sisters, it was customary for us to deliver and serve meals at the Priests' House. It was also customary for the convent kitchen to prepare special meals for the fathers. While the sisters ate turkey croquettes and Spam, for example, the priests dined frequently on steaks and roast beef. In every convent I lived in, when Father came to dinner, a special meal was prepared (with no expense spared) and all conversation centered on him. No one questioned Father's authority or disagreed with what he said. The author Lorenzo Carcaterra told the story of how growing up in Italy his father frequently brought the sisters hams, which they in turn always gave to the priests. All gifts given to the Italian nuns were routinely turned over to the priests. No one worshipped the ground priests walked on more faithfully than nuns. And given that general perception, one can't help but wonder what part, if any, sisters have played in the scandal and its cover-up. What part of the truth do we know? I wonder the same thing.

Sisters are seen by many as the mysteriously silent and submissive women in the church, and it's entirely likely that we know something that we're not telling. If anything sinister was going on in the priesthood, the nuns would have known. And since it looks as if the men in the priesthood have no intention of admitting the truth, maybe the women in the church, the "good sisters," will. We do know now that one reason many nuns keep silent is that they, too, have been victims of sexual abuse, exploitation, or harassment at the hands of priests or other nuns in the church. On January 4, 2003, Bill Smith of the *Saint Louis Post Dispatch* reported on a national survey completed by Saint Louis University in 1996, in which "'a minimum' of 34,000 Catholic nuns, or about 40% of all nuns in the United States, have suffered some form of sexual trauma," victimized by priests as well as nuns.[1] The survey represents the voices of 1,164 nuns from 123 religious orders in the United States. While the findings were published by religious journals in 1998, the story was never picked up by the mainstream press.

While I am totally shocked that nearly half of the sisters in this country have been sexually abused by priests and nuns, many aren't. On January 18, 2003, Mary Nevans Pederson of the *Telegraph Herald* (Dubuque, Iowa) reported in her article "Nun Sex-Abuse Does Not Surprise Sisters" that the sisterhood has been aware of the problem and has been dealing with it for years.[2] "This is not news to us. It's been part of our community history and we have dealt with it for a long time," said Sr. Dorothy Heiderscheit, president of the Sisters of St. Francis of the Holy Family in Dubuque. Other community leaders echoed the same message. And while some have interpreted the lack of publicity as a cover-up by the sisterhood, not so says Sr. Mary Ann Zollman, BVM, of Dubuque, and president of the Leadership Conference of Women Religious. "We weren't trying to keep it secret—it was published—but we were already aware of the situations in our communities and were responding wholeheartedly." As a group, the sisters did not see a need to publicize widely the information on the sexual victimization of nuns. Thank God the sisters are well cared for. The unanswered question is what happened to those who abused them.

Even though we continue to be stunned by silences we never knew existed, in 1996 those abused sisters began to speak. And while it took years for us to hear their voices, that's exactly what's happening. Maybe the silence that binds women deeply in the church will be broken by those in the sisterhood. Maybe the sisters, like more and more of the faithful laity, have also had enough. In 1986, Elie Wiesel accepted the Nobel peace prize and pleaded with us to speak up at times like this. "Neutrality helps the oppressor, never the victim. Silence encourages the tormentor, never the tormented," he said. When silence suppresses truth, only evil grows. We all need to look at the silence we keep. We have far more soul to lose in keeping silent than we ever do in speaking the truth.

When I looked back on everything I know about the priesthood, I feel as if I saw far more than I realized, and knew far more than I understood. As scandalous events continue to unfold, it's becoming clear that the crisis in the Catholic priesthood is far greater than just its pedophile priests. We're beginning to see a culture of privilege and sexual permissiveness in the priesthood that is as old as the church itself, and a moral theology that seems far more twisted than the most cynical could imagine—a spirituality so hypocritical in its obsession with and condemnation of the sexual sins of others, sins that now appear permissible only in the priesthood. Priests who engage in sexual relationships forbidden to the rest of humankind still stand before us as privileged "men of God," laws unto themselves, even holier than Thou.

As the crisis unfolds, we see far more than we ever care to and know more than we ever want to. The painful truth is just beginning to dawn. One by one we're beginning to realize how betrayed we've been by these "men of God." We've been duped into believing blindly in rules the priests themselves had little intention of following. And so many "insiders" describe the horror of what we see as merely "the tip of the iceberg." In the matter of knowing the whole truth, we've just begun. This is wake-up time in the Catholic Church at every level, inside and out. What the priesthood buried for centuries is being forced out into the light of day, as though the church itself has finally had enough. The sins of the fathers are being paraded before us today like those emperors with no clothes we read about as children. Only this time we see. And we see no longer with the eyes of children, but with the wide-open eyes of adults. We see with greater insight, knowledge, and understanding, and I dare say we are even finding divine strength hidden in what we see. We are not as shattered as we may feel. We are simply in the painful phase of becoming one, true church again, as we were in the beginning.

✝ ✝ ✝

At some level, the mystique of Catholic priesthood as a paragon of virtue faded long ago for me, as early as grade school. In this experience, also, I am not alone. For as long as I can remember, there has been a strange, silent acceptance of an unbroken tradition of sexual activity in the priesthood. The most common case in point when I was growing up in the 1950s: the live-in housekeeper who also vacationed and traveled alone with the pastor. Regardless of what we Catholics knew about the not-so-discreet sexual liaisons between some parish priests and some parish women, everyone pretended that nothing was going on. We simply didn't speak of it. That was true at our parish, Saint Stanislaus in East Chicago, Indiana, and true in the parish of nearly everyone I talk to. Somehow this pastoral partnership seemed unspeakable but okay. Never do I recall anyone, including my own parents, expressing dismay, disgust, or dissent. An occasional off-color joke about the special housekeeping needs of priests is the most I remember. We seemed to have no problem with priests who lived married lives, nor did we ever acknowledge the homosexuality of others. Ours was an acceptance so strange, so silent, and so Catholic that it included holding on to the church teaching that the priesthood was, is, and always will be celibate. That remains the church's teaching still, even though I suspect few priests practice it. We were given every reason by the priesthood not to believe that they were celibate, as were their housekeepers and lady friends.

In studying the history of priesthood in the Catholic Church, I see how celibacy was hardly practiced no matter what priests vow or what we're taught to believe by the church hierarchy. No matter how much the church proclaims the "unbroken tradition" of celibacy in its priesthood, all evidence points to the contrary, and not just in the eyes of a stunned laity. According to historian Garry Wills, over thirty years ago, in 1971, a very well respected American priest, Cardinal Seper, stood up before his brothers at the Synod of Bishops in Rome and reported, "I am not at all optimistic that celibacy is being observed."[3] The highest ranking members of the Catholic Church knew very well what was going on decades ago, as their recently released internal documents are beginning to confirm. Enforced celibacy never took hold in the Catholic priesthood; it was always mysteriously optional and never spoken about. That's why no priest is likely to accuse another priest of sexual misconduct and throw the first stone. As several "good priests" confided, "We all have skeletons in our closet." That's why we are where we are today, I thought, and that's how deep the silence is that the priesthood keeps. To reveal the whole truth would change the Catholic Church completely, inside and out. The silence is that powerful.

Contrary to what the Vatican would like the world to believe, sex scandals in the priesthood are not a phenomenon found only in the American Church. Widely publicized abuses have been reported in Africa (including the sexual abuse and rape of nuns), Ireland, Canada, England, Australia, South America, Latin America, and, if truth were really to be told by those who know, even in Italy and the Vatican itself. In response to my asking a sister who studied in Rome about sex scandals in Italy, she wrote:

> Just wait until things break in Rome!!! We think the pedophile and abuse culture is bad in the states, just wait until stories surface of folks in Rome!!!! The

priests sent there . . . plus the Italian priests . . . were not assigned there because they were saints!!!

American priests returning from Rome also shared with her their concern over the "rampant" sexual activity of Italian clerics.

What we see happening to the priesthood in this country is not an evil by-product of democracy, homosexuality, or a sin of the promiscuous sixties. Sexual permissiveness in the priesthood is as old as the church itself. All levels of the priesthood have been involved in the scandals and cover-ups—priests, bishops, archbishops, cardinals, even popes. The blessing of the Vatican rests upon them all, which is a clear sign of just how unfathomably high up the truth has been hidden.

In looking at priesthood from the beginning, I saw that the Catholic Church has consistently cultivated a priestly culture of privilege and permissiveness, with greater and lesser degrees of depravity and notoriety. Even with the beginnings of enforced celibacy found among the desert fathers in the fourth and fifth centuries, we find numerous, well-documented accounts of monks and monasteries with a wide reputation for molesting boys and seminarians, even engaging in bestiality. Sexual deviance entered the priesthood that long ago. Popes, bishops, and priests fathered offspring openly, with wives and children later sold into slavery, the rationale being that the financial upkeep of clerics' families would be too expensive and the church had no intention of supporting them or sharing its wealth. Therein lay the true origins of celibacy in the priesthood. Marriage for its priests would be far too costly to the Catholic Church. As the historian Elizabeth Abbott notes,"Bachelors leave no heirs, so would not be tempted to divvy up the property they administered, which would pass intact to the next generation of monks and churchmen."[4] Abbott writes of monks in France who were all married, and according to the abbey official Peter Abelard, each monk "supported himself and his concubines, as well as his sons and daughters."[5] These are just a few of the more egregious beginnings of the "celibate" Catholic priesthood. And if these sordid details are what passed the church's censors and were allowed into history books, I shudder at what didn't make it.

The Middle Ages were no less notorious for the rampant debauchery of the Catholic Church's popes, bishops, and priests. One twelfth-century bishop fathered sixty-five children (imagine child support!), and Pope John XII (955–964), known for adultery and incest, had no interest whatsoever in spiritual matters and died of a heart attack in the bed of a married woman. Some believe the woman's husband found them together and beat him to death. Most errant of the "bad popes," though, has to be Pope Innocent VIII (d. 1492). He was the first Pope to brag publicly about his brood of "bastards" and be forgiven by his priestly brothers for being so open and honest. Sound familiar? As much as we'd like to take comfort in the fact that this is now and that was then, I'm not sure that the priesthood today is much different than it was in the Middle Ages. What was called clerical concubinage in the Middle Ages appears to be an "unbroken tradition" still alive in the priesthood. It was still alive in our home parish of Saint Stanislaus, and nearly everyone I ask tells stories of places where it's still alive in their parish. We've always accepted priests who live married lives.

Few Catholics express grave concern over monogamous clerical relationships, least of all the priesthood. Most just seem relieved that it's not pedophilia or some other sex crime. We've grown so accustomed to that kind of spiritual hypocrisy that we no longer notice and rarely seem to care. While Catholics for centuries supported the church's teaching on priestly celibacy, we've also learned how to accept in silence all priestly evidence to the contrary. Only now are we beginning to see how devastating and deadly such hypocrisy can be for the priesthood, and the people as well.

One sexual activity that has never been accepted by anyone but the Catholic priesthood is the sexual abuse of children. Even the most silent of Catholic women knows outrage when it comes to child abuse. How could the Catholic Church and its holy fathers let that happen? How could they not see the clear criminal difference? And how long, O Lord, has this been going on in the priesthood? It's as though for decades, if not centuries, every priest who knew of child abuse chose at some soulful level to ignore it and let it be. In the real world that kind of thinking bears the criminal sounds of silence, so much so that questions are now being asked about the liability of those clerics who aided and abetted pedophile priests. The soul-stunning question for most Catholics is how our holy fathers could let this happen. How could the leaders of the Catholic Church accept in its priesthood a sexual deviance even the law of the land forbids? And how can they still not see, as the rest of the world can, the evil of their ways?

Even the most faithful and blindly obedient of Catholics dares now to question and challenge the priesthood because no one but the Catholic Church protected priestly pedophilia as if it were just another sexual practice to be overlooked. And no one but the Catholic hierarchy continues to behave as though nothing terrible happened, and to say that even if it did, the priest was not entirely at fault. The kind of thinking we hear today reflected in the statements of church leaders still reveals a quickness to forgive the priest and a persistent tendency to blame and overlook the victim. In the eyes of the hierarchy, the media bear major blame for inflating the importance of the problem. Every clerical effort continues to be made to keep the whole truth from being spoken. The only prayer we hear now from the priesthood sounds more like that of wishful thinking: "This too shall pass."

In trying to understand how this could have happened, I found myself returning to the beginning of priesthood. I suspected the roots of this scandal were deeply grounded; this crisis appears to have a very old soul, so to speak, as old as the Catholic Church. All the more reason to return to the beginning and examine how the abuse, the silence, and the criminal thinking started. What happened in the early Christian community that made "priesthood" and "church" necessary? And if an all-male celibate priesthood was the divine answer, what was the divine question? How did the Catholic Church become so obsessed with sex and when did its criminal thinking begin? Those are some of the questions for which you'll find my answers in the pages ahead.

Once it becomes clear how and why the Catholic priesthood evolved the way it did, it will also become clearer why we are where we are today. In looking closely at how the priesthood evolved, you may wonder more and more, as I surely did, how did we *not* see this coming? Given the history of priesthood, with its scandal and infallibility sitting uncomfortably side by side, falling apart this way was inevitable, as though destined to self-destruct with the same divine sword it pretended to live by. A priesthood that divided against itself simply cannot survive. What we see happening in the priesthood today is a mortal wound that is completely self-inflicted. That's the clearest sign of divine intervention I know, a sign that hidden transformational forces are at work even in all the silence we keep. God is with us.

1

Priesthood in the Beginning

When I returned to the beginning of priesthood, I looked first to the Gospels. As Christians, it's our rule of life as well as our beginning; and as sisters, the Gospels are daily bread. "In the beginning was the Word." That's how Saint John, beloved of Jesus, starts his account of the life of Christ. I see it as a divine hint of where we should begin our search, too. Especially since the first verse goes on to tell us point-blank, "The Word was with God and the Word was God." Which is like saying we can't get any closer to God than that. The words every true religion finds in their scriptures are the closest, most direct, and most inspired messages they have from their God. The Gospels are where the thinking of the Christian God can be found. That's where the divine intent behind everything can be found. And that's where I looked first to see what kind of priesthood God had in mind in sending Jesus Christ into this world. Because the life of Christ is God's divinely brilliant idea of what priesthood should look like, that's where I began.

Based on what we find in the New Testament—Gospels, Acts of the Apostles, and the letters of Peter and Paul—we know that celibacy and priesthood were holy and hotly discussed issues in the early Christian community. But the spiritual exercise of celibacy in priesthood is not new with Christianity by any means. Remaining unmarried in service of the deities is as old as religion itself. Virginity was always part of high priesthood for men and women, as is found among the gods and goddesses of ancient

Greece and Rome, as well as those of the Incas and Aztecs. Deities have always called single-heartedly a handful of men and women to do nothing but divine work on earth. Long before Christianity was born, virginity was an essential part of high priesthood.

Inspired as they were by the virgin deities of mythology, many ancient religions evolved with a sacred tradition of celibacy among their divinely enlightened leaders. The vestal virgins of Rome exemplify the extraordinary powers of celibate women. The Hindus even have a celibate god. In the Hindu community of deities, Shiva is worshipped as the god of celibacy and passion (creative power). Hindu ascetics vow celibacy in his service. Among Buddhist priests and nuns celibacy is also vowed, as are nonviolence and poverty. Buddhists believe celibacy to be the fullest expression of our highest state of consciousness. In other words, it's the key to everlasting happiness. The oldest and truest religions we know all seem to find a divine connection between the practice of celibacy and a powerful experience of God. All found some period of sexual abstinence to be essential preparation for communion with the gods. That's why celibacy became so important to the meaning of priesthood. Religious leaders were unable to discern the voice of God clearly without it.

In primitive religions, abstaining from sexual activity, temporarily or forever, was the most important way to prepare for communion with God in religious rituals. Similar to fasting in its effect, celibacy was experienced as a source of tremendously creative, even miraculous, energy and the most compassionate of loves. Widows, for example, were singled out in primitive religions as a mysteriously powerful group of women. There was something otherworldly about those who chose not to remarry, something divine about the independence that came to widows as they got their lives back. They were no longer "owned" by anyone, free in ways no other woman could be. Once again, or maybe for the first time ever, widows knew the joys of solitary splendor. And the longer they remained unmarried, the freer they were. In the early church, for example, they could follow Jesus and the disciples at a moment's notice, as many wealthy widows did.

Biblical theologian Elisabeth Schussler Fiorenza notes how, in the first century, wealthy women (many of them widows), were "notorious" for opening their houses to religious cults and their worship rituals. In the early Christian community, large numbers of wealthy women became their financial benefactors, as well as organizers and presiders of communities in "house churches."[1] The Emperor Constantine's mother, Saint Helen, is recognized as one such wealthy widow who devoted her life to promoting Christianity, and donated her money to relief of the poor and to the founding of churches on sites sacred to Christianity. While some question of authenticity remains, Saint Helen is associated with finding the cross on which Jesus was crucified, and in art she is depicted with the cross as her emblem. The unmarried status of women disciples is something Saint Paul commends often. In a letter to the Romans, Paul acknowledges as "fellow workers" the missionary partners Prisca and Aquila; women who not only supported Paul's ministry financially, but even risked their lives for him. In sending greetings to them in his letter, Paul asks "Remember me also to the congregation that meets in their house" (Rom. 16:25).

Saint Paul understood how invaluable the unmarried worker was in every Christian community. He also saw being unmarried as the perfect missionary lifestyle. In advocating celibacy, however, Paul makes it clear that he has no intention of placing restrictions on anyone. He simply wants to encourage what is good and what will help devote ourselves entirely to God (1 Cor. 7:35). In using widowhood as an example of the ideal lifestyle for discipleship, Paul explains that if a woman's husband dies, she is always free to marry. "She will be happier, though, in my opinion, if she stays unmarried. I am persuaded that in this I have the spirit of God" (1 Cor. 7:40). The divine connection between the "unmarried" state and doing God's work began to be wedded together in our thinking as Christians from the very start of the church, and most likely long before. In the beginning of priesthood, the unmarried become highly valued members because they are able to give their whole lives to the work of the church.

All ancient religions with a sacred tradition of celibacy have their priestesses, shamans, saints, priests, nuns, hermits, and holy ones. Always associated with celibacy are its divine powers and those who exercise them. Those to whom virginity is God-given seemed naturally (or supernaturally) capable of focusing their whole lives on creative work and lives of service. By sublimating in the divine all sexual energy, they seemed capable of finding all life sublime, even miraculously so. For example, among Christians martyred for their faith, suffering and death were actually experienced joyfully, as divine gateways to new and everlasting life. In the lives of the saints, it's those designated as virgins and martyrs who are most highly regarded as miraculous. One of the earliest is Thecla, a convert and companion of Saint Paul who was persecuted for "dedicating her maidenhood to God." Neither fire nor beasts could kill her. It's also reported that Joan of Arc, burned at the stake for witchcraft (hearing divine voices), never felt burned by the flames that consumed her.

A personal favorite is the amazing Saint Lucy. While few have confidence that the story is true, we were told that a young man lusted after Lucy so badly because her eyes were extremely beautiful. Rather than give up her virginity to someone who repulsed her, Lucy plucked out her eyes and said something like,

"If you love my eyes so much, you can have them." In art, she's often represented as dressed in red and holding two eyeballs in a dish. And in the story, Lucy's eyes grew back more beautiful than ever before. All of life is experienced as divine for those to whom celibacy is God-given.

✣ ✣ ✣

Side by side with the sacred tradition of virginity among priestesses emerged in some primitive religions an unthinkable (to me) but common practice among men to castrate themselves in the service of God—making castration appear the most supreme sacrifice in male "ordination." "The Church Father Origen; the obscure Valessi, a heretical Christian sect of the third century about whom little is known; and the thirteenth-century Russian Skopts are examples of these self-determined celibates."[2] So, too, was the leader and members of California's Heaven's Gate cult, all of whom committed mass suicide in 1997. While the women (vestal virgins, for example) seemed able to live without sexual relationships naturally, even with great peace and happiness, the only way the men could abstain from sex with just as much inner strength and confidence was to castrate themselves, to fix themselves in order to make themselves "men of God."

In male-dominated religions, it became a sacred tradition to literally cut oneself off physically in order to better serve God (and kings). And in doing so, a man established himself as holier than everyone else, even equal to Thou. If they weren't given the gift of celibacy by the gods, there were men who forced celibacy on themselves so that they could have access to its divine, even miraculous powers. And if the divine powers still did not rise within them "naturally," with castration, they ordained themselves with all kinds of exclusively male powers, the sacramental powers of the priesthood. From what I see, we haven't come far in our thinking.

Castration in the name of God. As though that would do it. As though virginity were exclusively a matter of sexual abstinence. And as though we can ordain ourselves men and women of God by literally cutting off sex forever. Who is that God? While castration was condemned by the early Christian community, the literal thinking behind it continued. To think that we would cut ourselves off physically in order to make "men of God" seems like blasphemy of the most profound order—not to mention clerical and divine deception, portraying oneself as a man of God when in fact one is nothing more than a man chosen by himself to be a priest. By taking the love of God in vain that way, what else could it be but supreme betrayal? Castration and forced celibacy in the priesthood appear just as abusive a practice now as they were in the beginning—so clearly man's idea of priesthood, not God's—at least not the God who gave us the priesthood of Jesus Christ.

If celibacy is not given to us by God, if it does not rise naturally in our lives through love, then there's nothing we can do or should do to make it our own, least of all castration. To think that we would take by force or create for ourselves an experience we call God's is blasphemy. In Paul's first letter to the Corinthians, he emphasizes that virginity is not a command, but a personal call from God, a different charism. "With respect to virgins," Paul writes, "I have not received any commandment from the Lord" (7:25). The general rule is that each one should lead the life God has assigned them . . . this is the rule I give in all the churches" (7:17). What happened to that general rule?

Forcing celibacy on anyone becomes so abusive that those who experience it that way become abusive also. Forced celibacy becomes naturally abusive, inside and out, because it doesn't come from God; it comes from us. The seeds of the abuse we see now appear to have been planted way back in the beginning of religion, when male priesthoods began making themselves into "men of God" through forced celibacy, even through castration. That was the beginning of man making God in his own image and likeness; and the beginning of priesthood's divinely "privileged" status. From what I see, that was also the beginning of the religious mess our world is in today. We still worship gods who hate everyone we do, and we're still hating and abusing one another in the name of our gods. We are still little more than haters and killers. After two thousand years of Christianity, it appears as though our minds have not changed much at all.

At least we know now that all the forced celibacy in the world can't make a bad man a good priest. That much is made clear in the daily headlines. There is nothing we can do to make one another "men of God" because virginity and priesthood aren't ours to give, take, or demand of one another. Taking the love of God in vain like that not only strips virginity of its divine intent and creative powers, but it devalues profoundly the loving experience celibacy is for those to whom it is God-given. We can see that clearly, too. The whole world looks at celibacy in the Catholic Church now and can hardly contain its laughter, or its soulful sadness. The oldest and most sacred tradition in religious life has become a big joke, and we're beginning to see why.

✠ ✠ ✠

The world Christianity was born into is not unlike the world we live in. Most of our world is male dominated, as it was then, and still violent, as it was then. The status of women and children in many parts of the world remains less than that of cattle, and the practice of slavery is nowhere near as gone as we may think it is. Even in the best of worlds, human life, not to mention all life, is not treated as sacred, even in the United States. The poor and outcast are not only still with us, but they remain just as despised and ignored, if not more so. The world we live in is very similar in thinking to that in which Christ was born. In many parts of our world, religion remains the major source of division, war, oppression, and abuse. The cradle of civilization and the birthplace of Christ are the world's bloodiest battlefields. Who is that God? For all that can be said truly of monumental human progress throughout history, we are not that well developed as human beings. In the name of all our gods put together, the whole world should know better.

The priesthood that Jesus brought into this world appears just as divinely fitting and troublesome now as it did in the beginning. In looking at the Gospels for insight into the priesthood of Jesus, it's important to keep in mind that the Christian Scriptures are not eyewitness accounts or transcripts of the life and times of Jesus Christ. The stories as we read them were written nearly a hundred years after Jesus' death and resurrection—one hundred years of stories and oral traditions being passed from disciple to disciple, community to community, town to town, and generation to generation. That's a long time to keep the original story straight, not to mention its divine intent. (It reminds me of the biblical version of the children's game Chinese Telephone.) Even so, the fragments that survived the years, through all of its translations, contain, as we Christians believe, all we need to know. Somehow the Word of God can still be revealed there by those who know how to listen, by those who know how to pray.

Not only do the Gospels reflect historical issues that were of divine importance in the early Christian community, but they also served as a source of daily inspiration and strength. In the beginning, the Gospels were the daily bread of the priesthood. Because Jesus lived those stories, there's a very real sense in which his Holy Spirit becomes present in the telling of them—especially when the community gathers around the table at the end of the day and shares stories of what happened. What miraculous events they witnessed. The crowds that followed and what moved them. Even what trouble they caused. All of which would have reminded them of Jesus. Disciples speak of actually feeling the warmth of his presence as though Jesus was right there with them. That happened frequently after the resurrection, where they say it "felt as though their hearts were burning inside them" (Luke 24:32). It reminds me of a line in one of Rilke's poems, "Imagining you my being burns more brightly." That's how real divine power is in the Word of God, and that's where disciples found inspiration and strength, daily bread and soul food.

Disciples felt divine power in repeating the words of Jesus, and they experienced divine power in repeating his works. The words and works of Christ are what define his priesthood. The table community is the real church of Jesus Christ, and all those gathered around the table are the people of God. In the Gospels, the priesthood of Jesus never gets more complicated than that. It's always a matter of doing God's work and being thankful for one another around the table at the end of the day. In the priesthood of Jesus, when that happens, God is with us.

Throughout the Gospels it seems clear that Jesus does not proclaim the founding of a "church" or "priesthood," certainly not another exclusively male priesthood. To the very end of his life, Jesus remained a faithful Jew who reveals no intention to destroy or overthrow Judaism. The synagogue remained the church of choice by Jesus, as well as the disciples, both before and after the resurrection. Jesus' priesthood does not come to destroy any religion, only to fulfill its divine promise. He envisions living our lives in an entirely different way, by the spirit of its laws, not the letter. The spirit of the law is God's voice. The letter of the law is our voice, our interpretation of what we hear God say, and too often what we want God to say. God sent Jesus into this world to return to all laws their holy spirit. And the life of Christ is what the fulfillment of all God's laws put together looks like. The one law governing the priesthood of Christ is love. Pure and simple, Jesus reveals that the only law of any true God is love. Compassion. Love is the priestliest power we have. That's God's message to the universe as revealed in Christianity according to Christ. And Buddha before him.

✢ ✢ ✢

One of the most profoundly misunderstood "priestly" gestures of Jesus is the appointment of twelve men as apostles and what that means about priesthood. By the end of the first century, the Church Fathers were proclaiming themselves direct descendants of the twelve apostles, and creating the teaching of "apostolic succession." The men in the church claimed the most powerful call of Jesus as theirs exclusively. Priesthood, they said, was intended, clearly and divinely, For Men Only. The Church Fathers found God's most divine blessing bestowed in particular on men, and mysteriously not as much on women. If Jesus found women equally as divine, they reasoned, he surely would have chosen them also as apostles. He didn't even choose his own mother.

Not only did Jesus choose men exclusively as apostles, but he chose just twelve. The literal-minded believe that means Jesus had no divine intention of inviting everyone to be an apostle. While Jesus may call many to discipleship, only a few special ones, "The Twelve," were chosen to be his "apostolic successors," his priests. As a result, the literal-minded also believe the "chosen" to be holier than the rest of us, closer to God, divinely privileged, even anatomically made in God's male image and likeness. Understood literally, that's how the division between priest and people took shape and became divinely ordained. That's how the subordination of women became divinely ordained. And that's when women were declared divinely unworthy of priesthood. As we now see, so clearly and so painfully, only evil and abuse rise from that kind of thinking because it kills the spirit of God. Jesus reveals over and over that is not what God intended. Divine spirits never speak literally. No one would understand if they did. We see that, too.

The symbolic ways in which Jesus reveals the love of God are intentionally those everyone in the universe can understand: stories, parables, miracles, works of mercy, and those divine gestures that are meant specifically to fulfill the law of God and the prophets. The baptism of Jesus by John is one of those prophetically fulfilling moments, as is his resurrection and the selection of The Twelve. Biblical theologians now recognize that the spirit in which the appointment of The Twelve is made reveals that Jesus accepts further his identity as Messiah. In picking twelve apostles, Jesus fulfills the Old Testament prophecy of the Messiah appointing heads of the "twelve tribes of Israel." Quite clearly, there is no priestly "ordination" going on there at all.

As Garry Wills observes, "Since there are no priests in the New Testament, there could be no ordination of priests."[3] He also quotes theologian Raymond Brown's explanation of what "ordination" in the early church probably looked like:

> A plausible substitute of the chain theory (of "apostolic succession") is the thesis that sacramental "powers" were part of the mission of the church and that there were diverse ways in which the church (or communities) designated individuals to exercise those powers—*the essential element always being church or community consent (which was tantamount to ordination,* whether or not that

consent was signified by a special ceremony such as laying on of hands). [Emphasis added by Wills][4]

In the beginning of priesthood, the Christian community practiced ordination by acclamation. In the beginning, it's the community that chooses and empowers its priesthood, and it's the community that ordains both men and women to serve in its sacramental ministries. Even so, the literal-minded still cling to the vision of a divinely ordained male priesthood and still claim the appointment of The Twelve as their infallible proof. (And *denial* still ain't just a river in Egypt).

Given the world in which Jesus lived, men were by law the only choice for everything in public and religious life. And by both religious and civil law, women were excluded from public and religious life. Because of the overwhelming biblical sentiment against women, the selection of men only by Jesus was a foregone conclusion. Nothing sexist or exclusive was intended: It was simply the law. No other credible choice could be made, especially because Jesus was fulfilling prophecy. *Woman* and *priesthood* were then just as cognitively dissonant to the literal-minded as they are now—and just as unlikely of happening. Understanding the fulfillment of prophecy as ordination to male priesthood remains one of the most misguided church teachings. And it is in such soulful violation of the Spirit of Christ that, according to Saint Paul, "There does not exist among you Jew or Greek, slave or free, male or female. All are one in Christ Jesus." (Gal. 3:28.) That's how the God of Christians envisions priesthood, "That all may be one." All.

While very early in the public life of Jesus there was a distinct religious movement associated with him and his followers, nothing about them claimed to become another church with another all-male priesthood. Quite the contrary. The vision Jesus consistently leaves in the Gospels is one of a church that includes everyone, and a priesthood that includes all who are called by the community to serve. The "unchurch" of Christ is what it looks like. It's like no other church in his world or ours, and what theologians call a discipleship of equals, a religious community bound by one spirit with many different voices, many different charisms, many different gifts, all equally divine in the Christian community. In the church of Christ everyone is invited to the table, and the priesthood of Christ is a calling every baptized person receives. All of us are ordained to do something divine with our lives. It's a vision of "church" and "priesthood" that remains largely unfulfilled more than two thousand years later.

Biblical theologians speak of Christianity's earliest beginnings as the Jesus Movement. Not a new church with its own priesthood, but a traveling community of Jesus' followers, distinguished in how they were governed: by love, by including everyone, and by a diversity of divine works shared equally by men and women. In the beginning, the Jesus Movement was seen as a religious-renewal movement within Judaism, aimed at correcting its abuses and relieving the oppression of the poor and the outcast. Maybe it was meant to be a divine renewal movement in all churches and priesthoods, aimed at correcting clerical abuses and aiding the poor and the outcast, once and for all. It was never intended to be a church, always a renewal movement within religion and priesthood. To me, the Jesus Movement became the most unchurch possible, and Jesus the most unpriestly priest. The visions Jesus reveals consistently of church and priesthood still seem unlike anything this world has ever believed in or seen. Thus we still don't know how to make peace on earth.

Unlike any priesthood, then or now, the priesthood Jesus guarantees heaven only for society's rejects, for three distinctly mentioned groups of outcasts: the sick and disabled, children and the desperately poor, and his favorite dinner guests—prostitutes, tax collectors, and sinners. Consistently, Jesus makes a public divine point of welcoming, touching, healing, and dining with those who are hated, persecuted, and condemned by everyone else. Those no one wants around the table, Jesus invites to be seated next to him. In the Jesus Movement, the last are always called to be first. The lowly are always raised up.

Not only do the last become the first in the Jesus Movement, but the leaders and presiders of the table community and the Eucharist become the ones who serve. And in every corner of every world, even now, who knows best how to serve but women? History has taught us that lesson for thousands of years. Women were servants extraordinaire, as well as constant companions and disciples of Christ. Because of how they were treated and touched by Jesus, theologians note that women and children were drawn in large numbers to the Jesus Movement. Wherever Jesus went, women and children followed. I see nothing in the Gospels that would lead anyone to believe that Jesus would exclude women from priesthood. In the Gospels, we repeatedly find evidence to the contrary. In story after story, Jesus breaks Jewish laws almost on purpose in order to make their divine point clear, in order to reveal the real intent of God. And in story after story, we find Jesus violating publicly (occasionally on purpose) society's and Judaism's most oppressive customs: breaking the Sabbath to heal the sick and feed the hungry, breaking nearly every law through the inclusive, even intimate, way he relates to women in public. It's as though there's some instant, intuitive, divine connection between Jesus and women. Nothing stops Jesus from seizing every opportunity to heal women, to free them, to save them from being stoned to death, even inviting himself to dinner in their homes. From city to city Jesus seeks intentionally the hospitality of the women disciples, finding himself at home in the company of those who believed in him. Just one look was all it took for women and children to see clearly that Jesus was God. As story after story reveals, it's the women whose lives were most miraculously changed and liberated by Jesus and his teachings. And it was the women who remained in touch with him, both before and after his death and resurrection.

The Gospel of Saint Mark (6:21–34) tells a powerful story of a woman with a hemorrhage, whom biblical society would have avoided like the plague and condemned as evil. After twelve years of expensive and unsuccessful medical treatments, she hears Jesus is in town and goes out to see him. The story says, "She came up behind him in the crowd and put her hand to his cloak. 'If I just touch his clothing,' she thought, 'I shall get well.'" And she did. "Immediately her flow of blood dries up and the feeling that she was cured of her affliction ran through her whole body." That's a miracle. Healing powers are revealed as primary in the priesthood of Jesus. We also read that Jesus is so powerfully moved by her touch that he was "conscious at once that healing power had gone out from him." Healers often speak of experiencing drastic drains of energy, much like that of a power surge. Jesus is described as feeling faint, "wheeling about in the crowd" and asking, "Who touched my clothing?" Somehow Jesus knows it's a woman and he goes looking for her in the crowd. Terrified, the woman throws herself in front of Jesus and confesses that she did it. It was she who touched him. Jesus tells her, "It's your faith that has cured you. Go in peace and be free of this illness." The moral of the story, Mark tells us, is that "All who touched him got well" (6:56). And what touched Jesus most powerfully was the extraordinarily moving faith of women; sometimes it even made him faint.

The New Testament is full of stories revealing how closely women were associated with Jesus, so close that women alone remained with him through his passion, death, and resurrection. The women did not run in fear for their lives and hide as the other apostles did, but stayed with Jesus publicly every step of the agonizing way to end at the foot of the cross. It was the women—Mary Magdalene, "the other Mary," Joanna, and Salome—who cleansed, anointed, and prepared the body of Christ for burial, and the women who were at the tomb first on Easter morning. Some believe they never left, but every Gospel tells the same story. Among all the apostles, the women alone remained faithful to the end, and ever after.

While the other male apostles were still locked up in hiding, the women knew for sure that Jesus would rise on the third day because the women knew that Jesus was God. Mary Magdalene was the first person Jesus went to see at sunrise on Easter. While we've been taught to think of Mary Magdalene as the world's most famous prostitute, nothing could be further from the truth. Biblical scholars found that Mary was an independently wealthy woman who supported financially the ministry of Jesus and was a close personal friend.[5] It's only through the sexist eyes of history that Mary Magdalene's "many sins" were interpreted as sexual because she was beautiful, unmarried, and wealthy. In the eyes of the biblical world, what else could she be but a prostitute? In the eyes of Jesus, she was the one who loved him most.

Mary Magdalene was first among the apostles to receive a vision of the Risen Christ, the first "priest" of the early church. Not recognizing Jesus clearly at first, Mary Magdalene, Saint John's gospel reveals, thought Jesus was the gardener, one who may have seen the body of Christ removed from the tomb and knew where they may have taken him. With her vision clouded by grief, it wasn't until Jesus calls her by name, "Mary!" that she knew instantly it was him. "Unable to cling to him as she wanted," she runs instead to tell the other apostles that Jesus is risen, just as Jesus asks of all the women to whom he appears. Mary Magdalene was the first priest of the early church to proclaim the Risen Christ, and Mary his Mother was the first priest of all, the first to give us literally the Body and Blood of Christ.

At first, the apostles refused to believe Mary Magdalene or the other women. They probably couldn't believe Jesus would appear to the women first. And they couldn't believe Jesus would ask these now hysterical women to deliver the news to them, The (fearful and trembling) Twelve. It was not until the Risen Christ passed through the locked doors of their hiding place in the upper room and appeared before them that the apostles began to believe. And only after they literally put their fingers into Jesus' wounds do they really believe without a doubt that he is risen and that he is God. This is the story's way of telling us how the literal minds of the apostles refused to change. Even after the death and resurrection of Christ, they could not believe it. The apostles still could not see with the eyes of soul, the eyes of faith. All four Gospels end with the Risen Christ appearing first to the women, then to Peter, then to the other apostles. If the literal-minded want to be truly literal here, the Risen Christ clearly gives priority to Mary Magdalene and the other women in the "new priesthood." The vision Jesus reveals is one in which priority is given equally to women and men. A vision of "church" and "priesthood" that is yet to be resurrected.

✝ ✝ ✝

The Jesus Movement after Jesus is the real birth of Christianity. That's when a religious community began to form around the profound personal impact of the Resurrection and Pentecost experiences, both powerfully life-changing (and probably head-spinning) experiences. In the descent of the Holy Spirit at Pentecost, everyone felt the divine power of Christ alive within them, so extraordinarily so that they began to speak in tongues, in languages everyone could understand: "each of us hears them speaking in our own native tongue about the marvels God has accomplished" (Acts 2:11). Those gathered were empowered divinely to heal, prophesy, forgive sin, bind and cast out demons, to do everything Jesus did. And all were drawn together daily in community for the breaking of bread. The table community remained Christ's "church" in the beginning, and all those gathered around the table remained his one, holy, apostolic "priesthood."

The only Christian "churches" that we know existed in the first few centuries were "house churches." Once again, the ancient religious tradition of gathering in the home for worship is by no means new to Christianity. This is not something the Jesus Movement or biblical theologians made up. The sacred ritual of a communion meal in the home of God's people is as old as religion is, and perfect in form for the early Christian community. The earliest days of Christianity were, as you'd imagine, taken up entirely with spreading the news that Jesus is God. Traveling missionaries, sent out in pairs, depended completely on the hospitality and support provided by Christian house churches, private homes designated in cities and towns as sacred places of Christian worship, safe and hospitable houses along the way where disciples were welcome to join the table community and stay as long as necessary.

Well into the third century, all Christian communities most likely organized themselves into house churches. Not only did the homes of Christians serve as hospitality stations and prayer communities for traveling missionaries, but some served as a kind of starter church in a new city or town. Houses were set up temporarily to provide space, support, and leadership for newly forming Christian communities. Paul's "fellow workers" (Rom. 16:3), Prisca and Aquila, founded and supported a "church in their house" (1 Cor. 16:19) wherever they moved. Gathering together in one another's houses for worship remained just as sacred to the early Christians as it did to Christ. The table community remained the church of Christianity in the beginning, and those gathered around the table remained Christianity's priesthood.

Given that house churches remained a powerful unifying element for the early Christians, we can be certain that the involvement and participation of women remained equally powerful. By both religious and civil law, the home is woman's domain, and in all male-dominated worlds home is the only place woman belongs. By law we know that women must have played a decisive role in founding and sustaining house churches, and in building Christian communities. And without a doubt, women played just as central a role in preparing for the Eucharistic meal, buying and cooking the food, preparing the table, welcoming the guests, serving and presiding over the meal, and cleaning up after. Given the strict traditional roles for men and women in biblical times, we can assume that if the community was gathering for worship in a woman's home, she would be in charge of everything. And at the table of Christ, the leader, the one who presides, is always the one who serves, most likely women.

I see every good reason to believe that women shared equally in all ministries of the early church, including what we think of as priesthood. In his letter to the Romans, Saint Paul commends most highly "our sister Phoebe who is a deaconess" (16:1) and "Junia . . . outstanding among the apostles and in Christ even before I was" (16:7). As co-workers and associates in ministry, men and women both preached the Gospel, founded house churches, and built Christian communities in every town they visited. Christians in the early church were committed to partnership in doing the work of the Gospel. The whole Christian community became an apostolic church in the beginning—one, holy, and apostolic—as the Catholic creed professes. Even with the persecution of Christians that went on simultaneously with all the missionary work, this was, indeed, the divine birth of the People of God, with a new heaven and a new earth, a new vision of church and priesthood unlike any this world has seen.

Not only did the early Church develop strongly as a "discipleship of equals," but we also know that within the Christian community, most in its priesthood were married. The Twelve were all married men and remained so, as did the early priests and bishops for centuries. Contrary to popular Catholic belief, in the beginning of the church there were always married priests. Virginity became advocated so fervently by Saint Paul (and many others) because in those days many believed literally that Jesus was returning soon. The end was near. And there was so much work to be done and so little time, especially for marriage and a family. Even so, everyone in the early church lived, as Paul recommended, "the life assigned to them by God." Everyone in the early church, married or not, shared in the priesthood of Christ. Quite clearly the priesthood of Christ has nothing to do with marital status, sex, or gender. In the beginning of the priesthood, all really were "one in Christ Jesus" (Gal. 4:28).

If you begin to think that this was heaven on earth and pure joy to the world, think again. Those who lived in Christ suffered everything gladly and did find a peace on earth that surpassed ordinary understanding. Everyone knew they were disciples of Christ by the way they loved one another, and in that regard it was heaven on earth. And they did bring joy to the world. But the early Christians still lived in the same world that crucified Christ and hated the Jesus Movement. The world was no less male dominated after the resurrection, and the only ones whose minds and lives were changed profoundly were those of the disciples, those in the Movement. If anything, the religious tensions that existed before Christ's death only intensified after: Christians continued to be persecuted and killed by religious and civil leaders all over for their revolutionary beliefs.

Some of the tensions that arose with the rapid growth of Christianity are those that come with every strong countercultural movement, especially if the movement is counter to male domination all over the world and counter to male gods everywhere. Equality and inclusiveness, the heart and soul of the Jesus Movement, are not only banned by divine law in patriarchy, but they're also condemned as evil by their God. After the resurrection, it became increasingly difficult for the Christian community to maintain its divine laws of equality and inclusiveness. And given that there's so little support for either today, you can imagine how forbidden both were, two thousand years ago all over the Middle East.

By the first century, patriarchy was already established as divine law and Christianity was experiencing the male-only pressure more and more profoundly. Open conflicts erupted over the role and participation of women at the Eucharistic meal. One fear was that the Jesus Movement, with its female-run house churches, was turning into a Feminist Movement, overpopulated as it was with wealthy, newly liberated women. There is nothing more destructive to patriarchy than the equality of women. And if anyone within the Christian community had visions of the

Jesus Movement becoming a "real church," as I'm sure there must have been, they would have been pressuring the community from within to move toward becoming a "real priesthood," a priesthood that looked and acted like every other priesthood in those days: exclusively male and increasingly celibate, a "discipleship of equals" no more.

By the year 110 A.C.E. (after the common era), the division between clergy and laity had taken place, as did the beginnings of a hierarchy of authority, previously unheard of in the Jesus Movement. The beginnings of Catholicism appear. The office of bishop was established as superior in divine authority to priests, who were superior in divine authority to the rest of us. Not only was the divine law of equality rendered null and void with the exclusion of women from priestly ministry, but so, too, was the divine law of inclusiveness. By the end of the first century, the "priesthood of the people" was well on its way to becoming the male-only priesthood of the elect; and with the male-only priesthood of the elect went all divine power and authority.

As Christianity grew to be a powerful spiritual force in the world, it experienced the pressures and desires to become a powerful political force, the most powerful church in the world. In a patriarchal world, *most powerful* can mean only one thing: an exclusively male priesthood that eliminates equality, and a hierarchy of authority and privilege to eliminate inclusiveness. The subordination of the individual to the church as an institution had begun. Conflicts over authority that had been brewing in the early church reached a turning point so momentous that by the fourth century Christianity became not only an official church but also the only recognized State Religion, and the Catholic Church became the only recognized State Church, now proclaimed the one and only true church—one, holy, now Catholic, and apostolic. In proclaiming itself the one true church, every other religion became heresy, anathema. Officially, all were no longer one.

With Catholicism declared as the State Religion, all other religions were removed by force. Pagan cults, goddess worship, and house churches were banned by law, condemned as heresy and as a crime against the state. Their temples were burned and ancient works of art, destroyed. For the first time, Christians began killing other Christians because of the extreme differences in their views. The church that was once so persecuted becomes the church of prosecution, and the priesthood of the poor and outcast becomes the priesthood of the rich and privileged. The crowning moment in the birth of Catholicism came with the appointment of Leo I (440–461) as the first "real" pope of Rome. Now the one religious leader in the known world, he was invested with all spiritual and worldly power. He became God and king in one man. It was then, whether we knew it or not, that the world was given a pope. To this day, every pope is envisioned as pope of the world, a law unto himself and in the name of God.

The betrayal we experience now in the priesthood began then, when being disciples of Christ lost out to becoming kings of the world. Divine power, which remained primarily an inner experience in the Jesus Movement, was not enough. It meant nothing in the real world. The literal-minded within the early church wanted real power, the power of money and privilege, the power to make laws and govern people's lives, the power other priests in other sects had, the power of patriarchy, the power of becoming divine laws unto themselves. As a result, and in the name of God, equality in the priesthood was subordinated to the divinely intended male-only tradition, and the inclusiveness of the People of God became the exclusiveness of the "priesthood of the elect." The presence of God was no longer celebrated in the home, but was taken exclusively into churches, by law now the only sacred places for worship. And even within their own church, the People of God were no longer seated around the communion table. By the fifth century, the priest, *in persona Christi,* stood on the altar alone, with his back turned to the people. Christianity's discipleship of equals, once recognized by the way they loved one another, became a house so divided within itself that it could not stand. Priesthood no longer came from the people, only from the elect. The Eucharistic table, around which all were welcome to gather, became the altar of sacrifice at which only the priest could stand. The voice of the community was silenced. The Holy Spirit present in the People of God became the exclusive property of the Catholic priesthood and the pope, the disastrous consequences of which become full blown in the Middle Ages. In looking at priesthood in the Middle Ages, we enter into the darkest soul of the Catholic Church.

2

Priesthood in the Middle Ages

IN ORDER TO UNDERSTAND what happened to the priesthood in the Middle Ages, we need to know about Saint Augustine (354–430), recognized as one of the greatest theologians in the Catholic Church, certainly its most influential thinker. More than any other Church Father, Augustine's writings most define Catholicism to this day, especially his teachings on the goodness of violence, the intrinsic evil of sexual pleasure, the seductively subordinate nature of women, and a law of celibacy in the priesthood—all of which contributed significantly to the decadence and depravity of priesthood in the Middle Ages, as well as to the problems we see in the Catholic priesthood today. For better and worse, the Church Fathers are still very much in line with the fifth-century thinking of Augustine.

Violence becomes part of the priesthood in the teachings of Saint Augustine. Among all Church Fathers, Augustine was the first to develop a theological justification of violence in spreading Christianity, the "just war" theory, making it a sacred duty to hate, torture, and kill "in the name of Jesus Christ." It's very similar to the concept of Islamic jihad. Forced conversions became standard during the Middle Ages. Holy wars against pagans, heretics, schismatics, and all deviants became glorious and triumphant works of God. The culmination of Augustine's blessing on violence "in the name of Christ" is revealed in the horror and evil of the Inquisition, as well as in the subsequent papal bans on dissent, including those we still experience. Hating and killing "in the name of Jesus Christ" becomes the papal blessing on all those who refuse to believe in Catholicism, including fellow Christians. It was a far cry from the priesthood of the Jesus Movement in which disciples were known to be Christian by the way they loved one another, not by the way they hated and killed one another.

The Catholic Church's obsession with legislating sexual morality also enters the priesthood with the thinking of Augustine. His most famous prayer appears to be the tormented prayer of the Catholic priesthood still: "Lord, make me chaste, but not yet." And while some church historians tend to minimize and even deny Augustine's obsession with sex, I find that his teachings prove otherwise. One has only to look at Augustine's writings (especially on original sin and the seductive nature of woman) to see that this is clearly a man who could not, without anguish, stop thinking of sex, and could not stop blaming women for his misery. Augustine fails to see as Jesus did that "the mouth speaks whatever fills the mind" (Matt. 12:34). "What emerges from within us, that and nothing else is what makes us impure" (Mark 7:20). It's what comes to mind that makes us clean or unclean. It's the way we think that makes us good or evil, and it's what comes out of us in what we say and do that makes us a saint or sinner. Action follows thought.

Augustine's teachings on the evils of sexual pleasure tell us exactly what filled his mind and what has filled the minds of Church Fathers ever since. The cornerstone of current Catholic moral theology on sex and the subordinate nature of woman was laid by Augustine. After more than 1,500 years, the Catholic Church still teaches that all sexual acts (even in marriage) not aimed directly at procreation are immoral, even intrinsically evil.

That kind of sexually preoccupied thinking, deeply rooted in Augustine's beliefs, became divine law with him and nearly every Church Father thereafter.

In Augustine's mind, man's obsession with sex has everything to do with the evil, seductive nature of women. Oddly enough, it has nothing to do with the truth, which is the sinful inability of man to think of women in any other way than as objects for sexual gratification. If that's not obsession with sex, then what is it? If sex is all that men see when they look at women, even children and total strangers, what else is that but a blind obsession with sex, a blatant refusal to see in others what Jesus saw, the face of God. Augustine's understanding of celibacy, therefore, is based not on a loving response to a profound experience of God, but on the sinfully sexist notion of woman as an evil to be avoided, a weak-willed, lust-filled seductress. So much for the revelation of Jesus Christ who reminds us repeatedly that it's what originates in the mind that makes us unclean. Evil lies in the eye of the beholder, and not in what the sinful eye beholds, especially not women and children.

If Augustine's thoughts on sex, celibacy, and the inferior nature of woman sound familiar, that's because they're all around us. To this day, the Catholic Church teaches and preaches that any sexual pleasure for its own sake is sinful and to be suppressed. Celibacy is still promoted, even in marriage, as the only way to avoid the seductive evils of pleasure-loving women and pleasure-giving sex. But what is as true today (as it was in the Middle Ages) is that even when there are no women tempters in the priesthood or in the monasteries, these "men of God" turn their sexual desires on one another, or elsewhere. Even in the absence of evil and lustful women, monks become little more than their own sources of sexual temptation, and given their sexually obsessive thinking, that comes as no surprise.

According to Elizabeth Abbott, so many monks in the Middle Ages resorted to molesting novices that it was said, "With wine and boys around, the monks have no need of the Devil to tempt them."[1] She adds that female donkeys were other favorites of monkish lust. In the sexually obsessed minds of the monks, animals were also seen as nothing more than objects for sexual gratification. As we see over and over again, it's what originates in the mind that makes us unclean. It's our sinful inability to see in one another (including animals) the presence of God. The cause of sexual abuse we see today is the human failure to think and see with the mind of Christ. We have no idea how to love one another, much less our enemies, animals, and the earth. We no longer know how to look at one another and see the face of God.

Five hundred years after the death of Augustine we can see the results of his thinking in nearly every Church Father after him. The tenth century in the Catholic Church is regarded by historians as the *saeculum obscurum,* the dark century, and the beginning of some of the darkest time Catholicism has ever known. Dark because it appears as though the popes, monks, priests, and nuns of the Catholic Church could hardly be more decadent than they were then, ruled as they were far more by the devil within than by the God of Jesus Christ. Medieval Catholic morality was just as obsessed with sex as was its priesthood. The whole medieval world in the West became possessed by daily personal confession and abusive physical penance, paying particular attention to sexual sins that ruled life both in and out of the monasteries. After more than five hundred years of soulful obsession with the intrinsic evil of sexual pleasure, the medieval church explodes with sexual immorality and corruption of every kind, much of which was centered in the monasteries and abbeys.

In the early Middle Ages, monasteries became the sole centers of learning, reading, and writing. Monks and nuns held a monopoly on education, giving them the exclusive opportunity to impose their abusive beliefs and practices. Double monasteries—monks and nuns residences connected by tunnels—were common at the time.

> In England, more than forty monasteries housing men and women together could be found between 1130 and 1165. In Germany, there was hardly a single house of monks without a nearby female house linked to it informally by exchanges of service and spiritual friendship.[2]

Apparently they shared a lot more than spiritual friendship. Double monasteries were eventually outlawed by the church because of the decadence and crimes that flourished there. Pope Martin V (1417–1431) shut down and prohibited double monasteries because they were too expensive and morally dangerous. As a result of the scandalous example of popes, monks, priests, and nuns, the whole medieval world exploded with sexual activity. So commonplace was sex in European monasteries that it became recognized as a way of life for monastic communities of nuns and priests, rather than a lapse of judgment or isolated incidents.

In Italy, for example, monks openly recognized and housed their concubines in certain northern cities, and in France, the monks of most abbeys were married. Medieval monastic life thrived on a culture of sexual permissiveness and privilege where homosexuality and the abuse of children were rampant, and in some situations probably believed to be divine, given the evil status of woman and the divine status of man. We will never know the true extent of the sins of these holy fathers, living as they did in the midst of obscene luxury, rampant and deviant sexuality, and every other vice known to mankind, including theft, forgery, rape, slavery, even murder. What we do know clearly, though, is that criminal thinking became commonplace in the priesthood in the early Middle Ages.

The institutional hypocrisy that began with Catholicism in the fourth century took full root in the Middle Ages with the total corruption of priesthood and papacy. This is the era of what historians call the bad popes, the errant popes, and the anti-popes. This is *centuries* of papal corruption, papal forgeries, papal battles and murders, and papal trials. And though celibacy was increasingly becoming law in the priesthood, the promiscuous sexual lifestyle of clerics persisted even at the highest levels of the Catholic Church, with no desire to reform. That's how powerful corruption is in the Catholic priesthood; it has no desire to change. And being *in persona Christi,* it has no need to change.

Among the many "bad popes" from which to choose, historians single out John XII (955–964) as the one guilty of the most grotesque debaucheries. E. R. Chamberlain, the author of *The Bad Popes,* writes that "John seems to have been urged toward a course of deliberate sacrilege that went far beyond the casual enjoyment of sensual pleasures. It was as though the dark element in his nature goaded him on to test the utmost extent of his power."[3] Chamberlain explained that John turned the Lateran Cathedral into a brothel, even stealing the offerings of the people for his personal use. He and his associates had a reputation for sexually assaulting women in the Basilica of Saint Peter, and he freely gave away church land and art treasures to his many mistresses. Not only was his sexual appetite insatiable and out of control, but so, too, was an inordinate fondness of gambling and torturing those who accused him of anything. "One had his tongue torn out, his nose and fingers cut off; another was scourged; the hand of a third was hacked off"[4]—all in the name of God and the Catholic Church. In the end, Pope John XII died in the sight of God just the way he lived, in the bed of a married woman.

While one would most certainly expect vigorous papal and monastic reform to follow as a result of such deplorable degeneracy, no such spiritual movement takes place within the priesthood or the papacy. And even though by the late Middle Ages the papacy loses all of its religious and moral credibility and opposition to the Vatican increased tremendously, Rome continued to block any major reform. Sound familiar? Even the Renaissance resulted in no rebirth of the Catholic Church. When faced with its own soulful decadence, the papacy continued to demonstrate then, as it appears to be doing now, no desire or inclination to reform itself, even to admit an error. The divinely privileged don't do that, they believe, nor should they have to.

On the contrary, the papacy did in the Middle Ages what it appears to be doing today: reinforcing the charade of perfect celibacy for priests, nuns, and all Christians; reinforcing blind obedience to the church and its priesthood; and continuing crusades to suppress, silence, and eliminate dissent. In talking with priests who recently returned from Rome (November 2002), a sister wrote about current Vatican efforts to whitewash the sex scandals:

> The situation over there is terrifying. The men in the seminaries are now walking around in their floor-length cassocks, hands folded in prayer, services in Latin, looking very pale and rigid. Rome is flying right back to pre–Vatican II and with it all the repression and mental illness that goes with this attitude. Very scary.

Nothing essential or substantial appears to have changed in the priesthood of the Catholic Church over the past 1,500 years. We are stuck in the dark thinking of the Middle Ages with no desire to think any other way because the Catholic Church can't be wrong. In the minds of the Church Fathers, that's impossible.

✢ ✢ ✢

Until the tenth century, celibacy, though rarely practiced, was primarily a monastic rule. A married clergy continued to flourish regardless of papal pressures to impose celibacy for all priests. But in 1073, Pope Gregory VII proclaimed celibacy for all Christians and a total priesthood of celibate men. Rome required of all clergy the renunciation of marriage and unconditional obedience to the pope. Even married couples were required to abstain from sex on Sundays and feast days, as well as on Fridays in Advent and Lent. I remember that rule. While celibacy became mandatory for all in religious life, the pope also decreed it necessary for the salvation of everyone else, married or not. The enforcement of celibacy turned up the volume on the need for blind obedience, both of which grew in importance, hand in hand.

By the thirteenth century, the thousand-year battle to enforce celibacy on the clergy finally ended in victory and became church law. In practice, nothing changed that much. The universal and compulsory law of celibacy was no more observed then than it is now. Neither priest nor people ever embraced the teaching as true, much less a law of God. What did change was the power of the papacy. While no one in the first thousand years of the church ever regarded the voice of the pope as infallible—obviously with good reason—the movement toward the absolute power of papacy proceeded by hook and by crook. Even in the ninth century, Nicholas I excommunicated anyone who disobeyed papal decisions regarding doctrine and practice. At the dawn of its darkest and most decadent age, the Catholic Church moved to centralize all power even in its most errant of popes. It was a kiss of death on the Holy Spirit who speaks in and through the people. Blind obedience became an essential part of the priesthood and the church in the Middle Ages. We Catholics have been blindly obedient for a very long time.

Obedience to God became obedience to the Catholic Church, which in turn became obedience to the pope. The pope, in effect, becomes God on earth, the infallible voice of God to be followed not only by all Catholics, but by everyone in the world. Thomas Aquinas (1225–1274), as influential as Augustine in Catholic thinking (including his disgust of women), is the first to proclaim unequivocally that obedience to the pope is absolutely necessary for the salvation of humanity. Along with the universal goal of perfect celibacy in the Catholic Church grew the universal goal of perfect obedience to the Catholic Church. While Jesus invited into his community all non-Jews, not so Catholicism, which demands unconditional acceptance of its teachings, always identified as absolute truth, divine revelation. And contrary to the sacred traditions of equality and inclusiveness in the early church, the hallmarks of the church in the Middle Ages were its Crusades and Inquisitions.

The Inquisition became an essential defining characteristic of Roman Catholicism, so much so that it was believed to be approved by Christ. And lest we think that this is something we've outgrown, think again. While the Vatican may be less physically violent with those who question its divine authority and teachings, the Catholic Church still deals in an equally despicable way with any criticism and dissent, especially within its priesthood and sisterhood. There is today a litany of those who've been "silenced" by the Vatican, especially those for whom the voice of God speaks a truth contrary to that proclaimed by the Catholic Church as infallible. Teilhard de Chardin was silenced for expressing his beliefs in *The Divine Milieu,* and Hans Kung has been censured for his writings on the Catholic Church. Within the sisterhood, Benedictine nun Joan Chittister has been challenged by Vatican attempts to stop her from speaking out in favor of women's ordination. Church authorities alone define all matters of faith and morals, and those who refuse to obey their "infallible" voices must be silenced. Who is that God? The Inquisition may have changed its murderous methods, but there remains an unbroken tradition in Roman Catholicism of suppressing criticism and dissent, especially that of priests, nuns, and all believers compelled to follow a divine voice different from that of the Catholic Church.

While the history of the church in the Middle Ages is one view of Catholicism, the history of how Catholics live the Christian life is quite another. Not everyone in the Catholic Church is as corrupt as its leaders. There always was and always will be those who refuse to obey any voice other than the voice of God, no matter how forceful clerical efforts are to silence and condemn them. Among popes, monks, nuns, priests, and laity alike there are always those who continue to live authentic Christian lives, uncorrupted by the hypocrisy and scandal of the institutional church. And nowhere is that glad truth more clear than in the Middle Ages with the rise of mysticism. The mystical tradition rises out of Catholicism's darkest ages, like a pure divine light that not even the most errant of popes with their most evil Inquisitions could extinguish.

The mystical tradition that became an essential part of priesthood and sisterhood in the Middle Ages is a clear sign of divine intervention. Regardless of what happens in the institutional church, there's a priesthood among the people that remains faithful, prayerful, and full of good works. When the voice of God demands something entirely different from, even contrary to, the "infallible" voice of papal authority, there are those called to follow the voice of God in conscience, regardless of the consequences. In the Middle Ages, mysticism appeared to many Christians as a prayerful alternative to the corrupt voices of Church authority. Even though Catholic teaching gives priority to the voice of individual conscience in decision making, the voice of the Holy Spirit within us, we are rarely encouraged to follow that practice. Another doctrine not proclaimed from the pulpit is the "doctrine of receptivity." In confirming the divine role of personal conscience, the doctrine of receptivity reveals that a church teaching cannot be true if it's not received as such by the community of believers, meaning all Catholics. While that seems like common sense now, how different Roman Catholicism would be had those two teachings ruled the Middle Ages, or the age we're in now.

Nowhere in history does the mystical tradition explode with such divine light and life as it does in the Middle Ages. It appeared to cut through the darkness and decadence of the institutional church, to drive many of its monks, nuns, priests, and laity back to their spiritual roots in God alone and the Gospel of Jesus Christ. Mysticism as a lifestyle is nowhere near as exclusive or as unattainable as it might appear, nor is it a divine gift given only to the fanatically religious. Quite the contrary. All ancient religions have their mystics and holy ones, including ordinary men, women, even children—like Bernadette of Lourdes and Thérèse of Lisieux, who became saints in their teens. The voice of God speaks in souls who listen, and not just those in the priesthood. Mysticism is a matter of being close to God, something everyone can be.

While the uneducated, medieval mind may be more naturally inclined toward mysticism than ours is, we, too, have access to divine revelation whenever we listen to the voice of God in prayer, see in one another the face of God, and see in our lives the touch of God. The twentieth-century mystic Evelyn Underhill wrote, "No deeply religious person is without mysticism, and no mystic can be anything other than a deeply religious person,"[5] which is to say a deeply loving person. We recognize mystics, those touched by God, in the same way Christ tells us we can recognize all Christians, by the way they—and we—love one another. Love is the infallible sign of all touched by God, and compassion is our most divine power.

Knowing what it's like to be touched by God is something most of us know. Anyone who experiences any part of life as divine knows what that's like. Anyone who falls in love with a man, a woman, a child, nature, or God knows what it is to be touched that deeply, that mysteriously, and that divinely. Mystics describe the experience of God as life changing, as one in which they undergo a conversion of sorts. Their whole life changes. As a result of being touched by God, everyday priorities shift and personal interests are drawn toward those activities that nourish the inner life: solitude, prayer, creative work, spiritual reading. Having been touched by God, we seek out the company of those also touched by God, those who are drawn toward lives of service, works of mercy, and creative work. All great artists are natural mystics. Emily Dickinson was, as was the poet Rilke and most artists I know. They have to be in order to move the soul of humanity so divinely and so timelessly. All those touched by God cannot help but be moved to works of love and works of art. Jesus reveals that "the mouth speaks whatever fills the mind," and if the mind is filled with love and God, life is filled with nothing but divine experiences. The writings of the mystics reveal how sweet that is.

What mystics tend to see more than anything else is the hidden side of life, the invisible movements of God behind everything that happens. Even in the darkest nights of the soul, and the darkest ages of the church, mystics experience the blinding light and love of God, along with the fullness of life for which we were created. All mystics write about how darkness and light are the same. One is not intrinsically evil and the other intrinsically divine. Both reveal divinely the dark and light faces and voices of God. In losing the taste for things this world offers as "divine," mystics write of experiencing all of life as sublime. All of life comes to the mystic as it did to Jesus Christ, as a daily opportunity to meet God face to face in everything that happens. Heaven on earth.

So powerful is the experience of God for mystics that even amid the decadence of the Middle Ages they speak of their souls being awakened by love, purified by love, enlightened by love, and inspired by love to works of mercy and some of the greatest works of art we've seen. Emily Dickinson explains it as "The Inner—paints the Outer—The Brush without the Hand." Living their lives in the presence of God, mystics hear divine voices and see the hand of God in the events of the day. They see things most of us don't. They are able to relax their minds and souls in such a meditative way that divine insights and truths come to them quite easily, insights and truths sometimes at variance with church teaching. It's no wonder then that the institutional church always regarded mysticism with mistrust—especially since women and ordinary Christians played such an important role in its development and since mystics tend to be strong proponents of holy disobedience. That's the clearest sign I know that mystics are touched by God. Women and ordinary people aren't excluded, and the only voice they follow is the voice of God, regardless of consequences.

Some of the most inspiring mystical writings are those of the women mystics. Teresa of Avila, a sixteenth-century Spanish mystic, is a personal favorite. In addition to composing volumes of inspired writings on the inner life, Teresa worked with her colleague and soul mate, John of the Cross, to reform monastic life in their communities of cloistered Carmelites. So rich is Teresa's inner life that she envisions the soul as an "interior castle" and speaks of her life as a union with God in a "spiritual marriage."[6] In understanding "marriage to God" literally, most nuns then wore wedding gowns on the day of their final profession of vows, and most envisioned themselves married to Jesus Christ. While I did not, many did, and I suspect some nuns still do.

I was told the story of a group of contemplative nuns who years ago understood the notion of being married to Jesus literally, in the sense that "Jesus" was the man whom nuns slept with at night. At their solemn vow ceremony, rather than lying prostrate in front of the altar during the Litany of the Saints (we knelt), they lay on their backs so that they could be impregnated by the Holy Spirit. It was a wise bishop who put an end to that practice in the abbey. Even so, while the image of spiritual marriage may sound like the revelation of a perverted sexuality, nothing could be further from the truth. It's purely a matter of a loving soul and the fulfillment of life that follows. All mystics speak with symbolic and poetic language, just as Christ did. Symbol, image, music, art, and poetry are all the language of the mystic, and are never intended to be understood literally. The visions and voices that mystics see and hear present themselves to us in timeless ways everyone can understand, except the literal-minded.

The fourteenth-century English mystic Julian of Norwich is another personal favorite. In her "Revelations of Divine Love" Julian envisions God as Mother and explains with pure delight how "Sin is no blame, but worship" in the way it can waken the soul to be touched by God. But sin as worship? No wonder the Inquisition harassed, tortured, and condemned mystics for heresy and women mystics for witchcraft, even burning at the stake women who heard "voices from God," like Joan of Arc. Anyone who hears and obeys exclusively the voice of God is asking for trouble in the Catholic Church. These are lives not dedicated in holy obedience to the voice of the Church Fathers, but dedicated in holy obedience to the voice of God heard in prayer and in one another, a divine voice we've been taught to mistrust and keep silent.

While crime and corruption entered the priesthood in the Middle Ages, so, too, did mysticism. Obedient to the voice and vision of God alone, mystics have always been a powerful influence in the Catholic Church. The soul of religion was kept sacred in their hands. It's the lives of those touched by God that saved the soul of Catholicism in the Middle Ages. And it's the lives of those touched by God through this scandal that continue to save the soul of Catholicism. The Catholic Church always was and always will be the whole people of God, faithful Catholics in and out of the pew who hold firm to what they know in faith and prayer to be true.

Even as the priesthood of scandalous clerics continues to self-destruct as it did in the Middle Ages, the priesthood of the people—good priests and sisters among them—will continue to be drawn by the voice of God in the Gospels, in prayer, and in one another, the Christian community. The darkness we know in Catholicism today bears all the divine power of a rebirth in mysticism, the likes of which we haven't seen since the Middle Ages. Taking religion back into our own holy hands is the first step. Moving closer to God in our hearts, our homes, and our families is all it takes for a rebirth of mysticism. Priestly people have always saved the soul of Holy Mother Church. That's another unbroken tradition revealed throughout the history of the Catholic Church, and never more clearly than when we look at what's happening in the priesthood now.

3

Priesthood Now

GIVEN ALL THAT HAPPENED in the Middle Ages (and not just what made it into history books), the fact that there still is a Catholic priesthood is proof in my mind of the hidden presence of God in the church and the survival of the Jesus Movement. It's a miracle. And we are watching it all fold and unfold right before our eyes. Something so painfully right appears to be emerging in the Catholic Church from all of its old infallible wrongs. Only a loving God could write so straight with such intrinsically crooked lines. What we're seeing today in the priesthood are those wheels of the gods that grind exceedingly slow, but exceedingly fine, giving us a new hope that the end of the wrong is in sight. This appears to me to be the end of Catholic priesthood as we've known it. All around us the high and the mighty of business and industry are being brought down by their own deadly sins, and Church Fathers appear to be lined up closely behind them.

For as much as we'd like to cling to divine comfort in knowing that priesthood today is nowhere as bad as it was in the Middle Ages, I'm not sure that's true. I felt I was in the Dark Ages when I read on the gossip page of the *New York Post,*

> WHICH American cardinal recently disclosed to insiders a confidential letter he received from a bishop urging the cardinal to resign for the good of the church? The cardinal is being urged to quit before his

> much-gossiped-about homosexual indiscretions are uncovered by the media. . . . WHICH ranking priest of a major diocese predicted over a boozy dinner the other night that if the media outs this particular cardinal, "then the dominoes will really start to fall?"[1]

Even though gossip is not always true, reading gossip about the Church Fathers in the *New York Post* is reminiscent of the darkest ages of Catholicism. But this is Holy Mother Church they're talking about "over a boozy dinner," not some clerical sex scandal from the tenth century. This is the twenty-first century. Do I know who they're talking about? No. But do the media, the priesthood, and the Vatican? I think they do. Apparently there are quite a few Vatican-appointed "dominoes" lined up and ready to fall.

The first truth we see when we look at the Catholic priesthood today is the way in which Church Fathers are making the daily news. That's the Catholic priesthood the whole world sees and knows. More hidden crimes and scandals being revealed, with more incriminating evidence that the buck does stop at the Vatican. All we see in response is the Catholic Church's attempt at whitewashing the issue. Repeatedly we are encouraged by the priesthood to believe that "this too shall pass." And it will—but not before revealing its darkest and most painful truths.

It's as though it's in fulfillment of Scripture, and clearly by the power of a very Holy Spirit, that the silence kept for centuries is destined to be spoken now, bringing all the dark deeds and deadly sins of the fathers into the light of day. "Nothing is concealed that is not being revealed, and nothing hidden that will not become known" (Matt.10:26). We were warned by Jesus more than two thousand years ago that this would happen. And even though it did take that long for us to see, we're beginning to.

I believe what we see in the Catholic priesthood is the beginning of the end. We see that the Church Fathers don't practice what they preach when it comes to celibacy, homosexuality, birth control, abortion, and all sexual activity outside marriage. Sex scandals and criminal activity continue to spin out of control, as does public ridicule of clerical crimes, now topping the monologues of nearly every talk show host. That's part of what we have to look forward to in the months and years to come. This priesthood has made of itself a laughingstock, and we are just beginning to see the heights and depths of the hypocrisy, scandal, and betrayal. And what's to come is likely to get far worse before it gets better, especially given what feels like the divine forces of Fate at work in the unfolding of events.

Every time I get news of another soul-stunning scandal, as happens almost daily, I can't help but feel that we are being touched once again by a hidden God. Some huge truth gets set free and some enormous evil once again becomes its own undoing. Everything that's been concealed is being revealed. So out of control is criminal sexual activity in the priesthood that they cannot help but end up in the daily news, not even while attending the pope's 2002 Summer Youth Rally in Toronto. The news from the end of the rally revealed two priests in their sixties from New Jersey were arrested downtown by police one night as part of a pimping and prostitution sting. According to church authorities, neither priest had a previous record. As one critic said, "I bet all the pedophile priests attended the pope's Youth Rally." I bet the same. If this is not the beginning of the end of this "laughable" priesthood, then what in God's name is it? When all the Church Fathers inspire today is anger, division, disgust, and ridicule, we can be absolutely sure that these are not "men of God" and clearly not the priesthood of Jesus Christ. The deadly sins of Church Fathers are being heaped upon all of us whether we like it or not, coming to us with the divine forces of Fate and all the signs of the hidden presence of God—and an angry God at that.

We are now all forced to see that sexual permissiveness and deviance has an old, unreformed soul in the Catholic priesthood. An April 2002 article by Maureen Orth in *Vanity Fair* on the indicted pedophile priest Paul Shanley quotes Richard Cardinal Cushing, who was at the time the archbishop of Boston and was leading a retreat for seminarians, that the theologian Fr. Richard McBrien (two years behind Shanley in the seminary) never forgot:

> Men, if you're going to do it, do it with a woman—don't do it with another man. And if you get her pregnant, come to me—I'll take care of it.

It appears as though the Catholic Church has a long Vatican-approved tradition of encouraging responsible sex in the priesthood. And it sends chills up my spine thinking of all the women who were "taken care of" in that way by the Catholic Church, whether by financial settlements, adoption, or priestly pressure to abort. It's a heart stopper and an eye opener for me, not to mention the women tormented by the church's teachings against them on birth control and abortion—mortal sins for women, not men, and clearly not for the "men of God" in the priesthood. I imagine Cardinal Cushing's fatherly advice is just a tiny glimpse of the teachings that created this priesthood, as we're beginning to see its criminally deviant results. With every new revelation of scandal, it appears as though karmic laws of Fate are indeed at work, some divine force beyond the church's control that's breaking the silence, some hidden God revealing painful truths that serve to set us free from the erroneous teachings of misguided Church Fathers.

For all who believe blindly that this whole mess is the result of the anti-Catholic media seeing things that aren't there and making up scandals, there's a growing mound of research that demonstrates this is no illusion. A vast majority of Catholic priests worldwide are living openly or secretly uncelibate lives. Data on sexual activity in the priesthood demonstrate what everyone seems to know and accept, but no one, especially the Vatican, admits as really happening. The Catholic priesthood is nowhere near as celibate as the Catholic Church still wants us to believe. It reminds me of the wisdom of *The X-Files:* Nothing is as it appears. But here we have statistics to prove it.

In 1990, a former monk and current psychotherapist, Richard Sipe, conducted a study of clerical sexual habits.[2] Believing the results to be conservative given what he knew, he reported approximately 20 percent of priests were sexually active with women, with another 10 percent thinking about it seriously. He also found 20 percent were homosexual, 10 percent of whom were sexually active, 4 percent of those with children. Some critics and seminarians, and most sisters I asked, felt the numbers should be doubled. Sex researchers also talk about the likelihood of an underreporting bias in sex research. So if you double the numbers, and add a little more for priestly bias, that's an overwhelming majority. Nearly every priest was sexually active or thinking about it. And that was more than ten years ago.

All over the world, research demonstrates that celibacy among priests is practiced mainly in the breach. In Brazil and Indonesia, where there is little cultural value to celibacy, it is more common than not for priests (60 to 70 percent) to have wives, lovers, and affairs. And in parts of Africa where polygamy is common, the burning question among priests is not celibacy, but limiting themselves to one wife. In Latin America, it's reported that approximately 80 percent of Peruvian priests marry or live with women. A Peruvian sister explained that many of those priests are missionaries who live alone in isolated areas and in another culture where celibacy is neither valued nor expected of priests by the people. The whole world sees that Catholicism no longer has (and probably never had) a celibate priesthood. All evidence points to the contrary. We can all see now that the mandatory celibate part of the Catholic priesthood has already changed, and without a Vatican Council.

Even more disturbing than what we know about the Catholic priesthood is what we don't know about the criminal and immoral activity going on. And the worst revelations are yet to come. If this is what we've been forced to know after decades, if not centuries of hidden criminal activity, can you imagine what we don't see and what we'll never know? If this is what court-ordered documents reveal, imagine what must have been shredded and destroyed. Out of everything we see in the priesthood, the silence priests are bound to keep is the deepest kiss of death, full of the unwillingness to change anything, especially their minds and their privileged unpriestly lives. At a time when the whole world looks at the Catholic priesthood with outrage, Church Fathers appear to wrap themselves in the silence of the brotherhood, offering heartfelt apologies void of the whole truth and pastoral advice to "weather the storm" and "move on." The silence demanded by the Church Fathers in the face of their crimes and misdemeanors is the most disturbing silence of all. If we decide to keep it.

Garry Wills writes in depth about the institutionalized "conspiracy of silence" that exists from pope to priest, and most likely as well to bankers, lawyers, judges, law enforcement, and media. Aiders and abettors galore swirl around this scandal, and more silence than we'll ever know is being kept criminally safe by them, too. It looks as if a very highly organized system of protection and silence has been smoothly operating in the Catholic Church for a very long time. Wills calls them structures of deceit, building blocks of the priesthood. That's not being sarcastic. That's the only way any of this could possibly happen and stay so hidden for so long—plenty of high-powered help, both in and out of the Catholic Church, from the very start. "Keeping the silence" has all the markings of the Inquisition of the twenty-first century. In the name of God (and not spreading the scandal) the Church Fathers demand blind obedience to everything they ask, and forbid its priests from breaking the silence of the brotherhood. The unbroken tradition of keeping priestly silence rules: No dissent allowed.

One deadly sound of silence so striking in the priesthood is that of its priests, good ones included, who aren't telling everything they know. It feels criminal to see how claims of abuse remain the burden of the victims and their families. I've yet to hear more than a handful of reports by brother priests, superiors, or communities coming forward first to spare victims further anguish. Certainly, priests must know who their pedophile brothers are. Everyone else seems to. The *Boston Globe* knows. The *New York Times* knows. And the *National Catholic Reporter* makes sure Catholics know. All over the world reports of abuse continue to be made public, but not yet from within the priesthood or the Catholic Church. Clerical lips remain sealed regardless of new zero-tolerance policies, and the unwillingness to be absolutely truthful only intensifies. Minds that haven't changed for thousands of years are not likely to be moved by new rules and guidelines.

In the silence kept by the priesthood, what we see is an inability to change its ways of thinking, its criminal and immoral ways of acting, its refusal to change in any way at all. We see a refusal even to admit that we are now a house so corrupt within that the Catholic Church cannot exist as it is much longer. The People of God cannot stand it as it is much longer. We are seeing that happen in Boston, in New York, and in Los Angeles. If it's not happening in your home town, do not for one second believe that it's not a problem. In a survey conducted by the *New York Times*, reporter Laurie Goodstein writes of how the "Trail of Pain in Church Crisis Leads to Nearly Every Diocese."[3] Every region of the country was seriously affected, "with 206 accused priests in the West, 246 in the South, 325 in the Midwest and 434 in the Northeast." This is the Body of Christ we are talking about, and if one of its vital organs is terminally diseased, then the whole body is dying, whether the pain has hit or not. It's just a matter of time.

It does not appear as though the priesthood can reform itself today any more than it did in the Middle Ages. The church leaders have yet to see the problem. What we're likely to see instead of real progress is what we've known all along: denial, denial, denial—possibly with better behavior, though that remains to be seen. The most blatant cases of abuse are still being fought in court and resisted by the church. (When it comes to the sexual abuse of children, there is no such thing as statutes of limitations.) Evidence is hidden and suppressed, if not destroyed, and justice is being obstructed by those who are quickest to condemn injustice in everyone else. Acting as a law unto itself, the Catholic Church's defiance of the civil laws of the land continues as though there is no problem at all, certainly not as big as the one I see.

The inability to change is the clearest sign we know of predictable corruption and death. Whatever doesn't grow and change dies naturally. Natural death by corruption and decadence appears to be part of the transformation at work in the priesthood today. By forces clearly beyond anyone's control, the conspiracy of silence that binds the priesthood has finally become its own soulful undoing. With divine forces of Fate coming to meet them, the silence that so many victims swore to God to keep is being moved fearlessly to speak, moved to tell the horror of what their kept silence concealed, moved to speak the unspeakable. In one way or another, the truth is being set free.

As above, so below. Given all the chaos and crisis we've seen, imagine all the hidden chaos and crisis that we can't see. Given all the closed meetings, doors, and sessions, we can tell that great efforts are being made to keep a growing number of clerical lids on, even though within the priesthood the conspiracy of silence appears ready to blow its top. We are hearing a growing number of "anonymous" voices from the priesthood, revealing dissent, discouragement, even disgust, as though they can hardly stand themselves or what's happening. A priesthood that is so divided within itself that it, too, can hardly bear another scandal, another revelation of some damning truth. We are beginning to hear from the priests who can't stand it anymore, thanks in part to the *National Catholic Reporter*, an independent newsweekly that consistently honors as sacred all voices of dissent.

One section of the October 11, 2002, issue of the *NCR* reveals what a colossal mess there is among priests and people in the Los Angeles archdiocese. The headline of the article by Arthur Jones reads "Discontent and Disaffection Grow as L.A. Archdiocese Dismantles Ministries."[4] I see the words *discontent* and *disaffection* and automatically I feel the presence of God. The story is about further sex-abuse indictments in the archdiocese topped off with the dedication of a brand new $190 million cathedral, followed immediately thereafter with the "dismemberment" of traditional Catholic ministries, for financial reasons. The list of programs axed by Archbishop Roger Mahoney reads like a Litany of Services Dead in the Catholic Church:

Campus Ministries
Prison Ministries
Minority Ministries (Asian, Hispanic, African-American)
Disabled Ministries
Gay and Lesbian Ministries
Interfaith Ministries
Pro-life Ministries

If that isn't a litany of a dead priesthood, then what is it? In a priesthood of privilege, social justice is the first to go.

No wonder good priests are barely surviving and are ready to explode (and we need to wonder seriously about those who aren't). Who with the mind of Christ could look at the behavior of this priesthood and not explode in anger and disgust? Speaking anonymously, one L.A. priest described what he sees going on: "I think increasingly the priests are coming to a more critical stance. There is a universal perception that as an archdiocese we're in tremendous disarray right now." A more outraged L.A. priest wrote an anonymous letter to the *NCR* voicing "unanimous" priestly sentiment against Archbishop Mahoney, who they feel "sold us down the river to save his own episcopal ass."[5] Both voices give us a pretty clear picture of what life must be like within the priesthood. Quite clearly, they cannot keep silent much longer.

Priestly voices of dissent, like those of the laity, grow louder and clearer with each scandal. Anonymous though these voices are, this is just the beginning of the end to the silence priests keep, the beginning to the end of the way they are. It has to be. All the signs of the time point to the end of Catholic priesthood, and with all the divine forces of Fate making this priestly transformation happen. Enrollment in the priesthood continues to nosedive, morale couldn't be lower, public perception couldn't be worse, and even if you were interested in priesthood, what thinking person would join now, man or woman? Given what we see brewing in Los Angeles, Boston, and New York City alone, we know things are going to get a whole lot worse before they get better. The death of this priesthood, unlike its life, is clearly not happening in silence.

The crisis, chaos, and dissent we're beginning to see and hear in the priesthood are clear signs of the presence of God. Any true God would be outraged by the crimes, the hypocrisy, the scandal, and betrayal of these "men of God." And I would die of despair (not really) if someone in the priesthood wasn't disgusted over what his brethren had turned this Catholic Church into. The growing voice of anger and dissent rising among priests is the clearest sign we have that something divinely fitting, right, and just is emerging in this priestly mess. It was the priests of Boston whose dissenting voice ordained the removal of Cardinal Bernard Law as archbishop. Even the brotherhood is growing outraged and restless, and it's only a matter of time before everything becomes undone, before all those "dominoes" really begin to fall (and all those priestly fingers start pointing at one another). It's part of the wisdom of hidden gods that we are given no more truth than we can handle at any one time, even though it may feel like we've already had enough.

If we are looking for the hand of God in this holy mess, I see it in those anonymous voices of priestly dissent, "men of God" who have had enough of the scandal, hypocrisy, and betrayal. Those who remain silent, even the "very best" of them, are the ones I question; they remain stumbling blocks to revealing the whole truth, as do their supporters. A friend told me about a "fabulous" priest in her parish who was "like a sex addict." She said, "Just because he can't keep it in his pants doesn't mean he can't be a good priest." I thought it did. While *priest* and *sex addict* are still cognitively dissonant to most, in the most educated Catholic mind they make sense. That's how skewed our understanding of priesthood has become, and that's how low our standards and expectations of priesthood have sunk. The number of "fabulous" priests who have something to hide appear to be legion, as do their accomplices.

Along with the priestly voices of dissent and disgust, it's no small comfort for Catholics that we have holy beginnings, we have Scripture to turn to, reminding us that the God of Jesus Christ also holds in horror those priests who turned away so many with their scandal and hypocrisy. Jesus calls these priests a "brood of vipers, whitewashed tombs, and frauds." "You present to view a holy exterior while you are full of hypocrisy and a secret rottenness" (Matt. 23, 27). And to those who show scandal? There is no room whatsoever in the priesthood of Christ for them. "Woe to whoever scandalizes the little ones. It is better for him that a millstone be hung around his neck and he be drowned in the depths of the sea" [not readmitted to priesthood] (Matt.18:6). While our hearts may be troubled and afraid by what we see happening in the Catholic Church, we have God's Word that the Holy Spirit of truth is always within us, far more powerful and freeing than the silence we keep. That's a promise.

The voices of dissent that we hear in the priesthood and in the people are the clearest voices of God I know. And the voice of God we hear in Scripture is the clearest call to the priesthood of Christ I know. While we have hardly begun to understand the ways in which we've been victimized and betrayed by the Church Fathers, enlightenment will come as a newly transformed priesthood rises from the people again and moves forward. What is most true and divine about Catholicism can never die. What's true about any religion can never die. True gods can be buried for centuries in hypocrisy, crime, and scandal, but they can never be killed, no matter how decadent and deadly silent their priesthood. That's been infallibly true in the Catholic Church for more than two thousand years.

From what I can see of the priesthood, this is just the beginning—the beginning of the end to the criminal thinking and hypocrisy, as well as the emergence of a new priesthood in the Catholic Church. There are already millions of Catholics—good priests and sisters among them—who always have and always will protect and preserve the truth like the Word of God that it is. It's those Catholics faithful to the truth who have always held together Holy Mother Church, and it's those faithful Catholics who hold her together now when she seems to be falling apart. All those touched by God through this crisis, both in and out of the pew, are leading the way. We have good reason to believe that God is with us. No matter what stunning truths are revealed to us in the months and years to come, the priesthood of the people has come alive in ways the Catholic Church has never seen in its history—"A Death Blow is a Life blow to Some." Just as we are witnessing the transformation of priesthood by the people in the Catholic Church, so, too, are we beginning to witness the transformation of sisterhood by women in the Catholic Church.

PART TWO

Sisterhood

Introduction

ONCE A DISCUSSION OF the "big priest scandal" winds down, the next question I am asked, oddly in a more subdued, almost reverent tone of voice, is "What's going on in the sisterhood?" Are nuns just as sexually active as priests? Is celibacy as ignored in the sisterhood as it is in the priesthood? Are nuns abusing children sexually, and are we hiding, protecting, and supporting them, too? Those of you who work with us, play with us, pray with us, and know us so well, do you see a culture of privilege and rampant sexual activity in the sisterhood? Are the media just missing "the nun story"? Is there any evidence at all that a big nun scandal is brewing and about to blow wide open any day?

As a sister for forty years, I haven't seen any of that at all. But I didn't even know 40 percent of American Catholic nuns are victims of sex abuse by priests and sisters. Just because we don't see in the sisterhood the excesses of sexual activity and cover-ups that we see in the priesthood doesn't mean the sisterhood has been void of sexual activity and sexual abuse or is not prone to secrecy and cover-ups. Nothing can be further from that truth, as history serves divinely to remind us. Whenever religious life and celibacy are not freely chosen, hidden sexual activity and abuse (though women rarely become pedophiles) will be found. Once celibacy becomes forced, the chain of sexual abuse has begun; we force ourselves to think and act in ways that are contrary to how we feel. It's a divine law of human nature that the more sexual activity feels prohibited, the more it goes underground and flourishes, wrapping us in deadly silence. According to Carl Jung, "Whatever we don't bring to consciousness comes to us as Fate." The exact opposite happens every time celibacy is forced on those who don't want it, nun, priest, or anyone else.

But even if you add up the incidents in history of sisters having sex with priests, one another, or anyone else, it will never come close to the culture of privilege and sexual permissiveness that exists in the priesthood. Why not? Because while celibacy is experienced by most priests as an enforced rule (though not really), it's welcomed freely as a divine way of life by women in the sisterhood. There's nothing forced or oppressive about celibacy for the sisters I know. Quite the contrary. Most of us can't imagine living happily any other way. With all due respect to marriage, children, and even sexual liaisons, every sister I know prefers the solitary splendor and divine freedom that come from within a celibate sisterhood. Unlike the priesthood, which has resisted celibacy for two thousand years, the sisterhood embraces the vow as its heart and soul. In the priesthood, celibacy is all about sex and sacramental powers; in the sisterhood, celibacy is all about the experience of God and the call to lives of service.

For centuries, nuns have been seen—correctly—as the silent, submissive women of God, called on to do the church's works of mercy: the compassionate works of nursing, teaching, community service, and caring for everyone who calls, Catholic or not, friend or enemy. It was the Church Mothers, not the Church Fathers, who really educated us as Catholics and taught us to pray. Nuns were the ones who introduced us to God and the power of prayer before we could read. They were the ones who cultivated the feasts of the saints and introduced us to their miraculous lives. At the age of five we were taught by these mysterious women to believe that we were surrounded by saintly spirits and carried God within us wherever we went. While the priest displayed his divine powers daily on the altar, it was the sisters who cared for our hearts and souls. While the Church Fathers may have been the official ordained representatives of God, the Church Mothers were God's sisters and angels of mercy. Sisters made me the Catholic I am today.

At Saint Stanislaus School in East Chicago, Indiana, nuns were far more a part of our daily lives than priests ever were. In the 1950s, the Sisters of Saint Joseph (Third Order of Saint Francis) not only educated us, but they also helped raise us. In those days, Catholic schools were run by the sisterhood, which meant that we literally spent more of our waking hours with sisters than we did with our own families. Nearly eight hours a day, five days a week, nine months a year for nine years, each day began at 8:00 A.M. with mass and Holy Communion under the constant guidance and close supervision of the Sisters of Saint Joseph. For nine of our most formative years we were surrounded by nuns. I remember a very big sister telling us early in life, "Children, never forget that we nuns are like God. We are everywhere." And they were, often appearing silently out of thin air. Obviously I never did forget.

While occasionally terrified by what we now recognize as physical abuse (I, too, got knuckle-whacked by a sister with a steel-edged ruler), I was always one of those Catholic girls to hang around after school, and not because I had to. Veronica Hargrove (my best friend still) and I stayed after school nearly every day to help Sister clean the classroom, but even more so to get a breathtaking religious prize for volunteering—such as the praying statue of Mary as a little girl, which we believed to be magic, and the floating Blessed Mother pen, which I still have. I was a friend (as was my family) with nearly every sister I knew in grade school and high school, yet never was there even a hint of anything sexual, not toward me or any of my friends. I can't think of a single nun who made us feel uncomfortable in a sexual way.

For as close as we felt to the nuns who taught us, and for as much time as we spent with the sisters both in and out of class, never did any of us see the inside of the convent, much less spend the night there regularly (as victims did with pedophile priests in the rectory). Outside of class, there was no contact with nuns in grade school, and not that much in high school. At the end of the school day, it looked as if the sisters were locked up in the convent for the night, not appearing again in public until morning. We never knew what nuns did behind convent doors. That was the greatest mystery of all.

Only a few of us saw the inside of the convent, and when we did, it nearly made the school newspaper. We never saw anything other than the parlor or kitchen, and only for a split second (we were never allowed to sit down). Because my family owned the neighborhood Normal Bakery (that was its name), I got to see the convent kitchen several times. Whenever my dad donated cakes and "buns to the nuns," the cook sister had us deliver them right into the kitchen. She also slipped sticky unwrapped hard candy into my coat, making it inedible with pocket fuzz. Only once did I get anything edible from her: a boring apple one Halloween. Maybe that's why I can't remember her name.

I heard a similar story from a nun who in grade school was brought into the convent parlor with a few other girls (never boys) for a well-deserved treat. Telling the girls not to sit down, Sister disappeared briefly and returned with a jar of peanuts and measuring spoons. Each girl held out her hand, got one tablespoon of peanuts, and then was told to leave. That's how laughably limited contact was between nuns and girls while the sexual abuse was going on between priests and boys. The chance of contact with nuns outside the classroom was nonexistent. Even those of us who joined the sisterhood at the age of eighteen never saw the inside of a convent until after we entered—at least nothing above the main floor, and only those areas designated as communal (parlor, chapel, dining room). Recently I asked my best nun friend, Holy Cross Sister Mary Ann Pajakowski, if she ever spent time inside the convent before joining. In return I received a very funny e-mailed response:

> I think I was in our grade school convent twice—once to eat burned apple slices in the parlor which was a treat for three of us girls who got pulled out of school to clean church, and the other time was when the same three of us were pulled out of school to throw out the very dry Christmas tree for the nuns—it was so dry that we didn't want to carry it out and clean up the needles, so we pushed it out the third floor window and of course got hollered at blah blah blah. So for 9 years of Catholic school that was it. Only one time in high school, and that's because I tripped and skinned my knee in the summer and cleaned it up in the parlor of Saint Joe High. One other time was when Sister Octavia measured me for the hem of my postulant skirts—she was put out because my hips were crooked and she had to pin all the way around.

Such is the extent of the personal contact girls had with nuns in and out of the convent. What this goes to show is how profoundly different sisterhood is from priesthood, inside and out. Our religious and community lives are lived in an entirely different manner.

As we look at sisterhood in the beginning, in the Middle Ages, and now, it will become clear how differently celibacy is experienced by men and women in general, priests and sisters in particular. In the priesthood, we saw celibacy emerge in the fourth century with the force of a no-sex rule for already married priests, and today we witness daily the disastrous results of that misguided kind of thinking. The history of celibacy in the priesthood appears as one of nothing but enforced failure. Celibacy never works as a rule because that's not what it is and that's not its divine intent. Nothing can be further from celibacy's divine truth than a no-sex rule. That is celibacy at its crudest.

For the women in the early church, however, who by the fourth century were pretty much squeezed out of Christianity's priesthood, celibacy emerged as the sacred key to an apostolic lifestyle. For the Church Mothers, celibacy had everything to do with the complete freedom necessary (like that of every man) to pick up and go with the apostles. Celibacy provided our first sisters with the freedom they needed, inside and out, to continue doing the priestly works of Christ, "ordained" or not. While for men in the priesthood celibacy became the great oppressor, for women in the sisterhood celibacy became the great liberator, the great equalizer within Christianity. Being excluded from priesthood never stopped the Church Mothers from doing apostolic works. No one or nothing could stop the sisterhood from living priestly lives because they, too, were touched and called by God.

When freely chosen and gladly welcomed, celibacy in the sisterhood has everything to do with how powerfully a handful of women experience God and how totally liberating the experience is. So much so that priorities shift and interest becomes lost in everything but tending to lives of service, keeping the divine fires burning, keeping Holy Mother Church alive and well. Other than the work of making life divine, nothing matters in the sisterhood, least of all sexual liaisons. God-given celibacy emerged as a liberating priestly power among women in the early church, as it does now. It was experienced as a divine energy, a creative power that couldn't be taken away, denied, or silenced. It's still true that everything else in life pales in comparison to what women find in celibate sisterhood.

For example, most sisters I know don't care who makes the most money; who has the most prestigious job; who is the skinniest, most stylish, smartest, or most attractive. Nor do we believe the one who dies with the most things wins. Sisters I know take exception to all the ways in which women and men are preoccupied with privilege, with competing and outdoing one another. Everything about us tends to be countercultural in that way, including the relatively plain way we look, in or out of habit. (Regardless of what we wear, my sister Debbie swears she can spot a nun in any crowd.) From what I can see, all that matters in the sisterhood is how free celibacy leaves us, inside and out, to be sisters (and priests) in all the ways we can. And from what I've experienced, all that matters is how sweetly celibacy binds together women as sister, leaving us with the pure pleasure of one another's company and all the pure joys of sisterhood.

Too hard to believe? Too good to be true? Yes and no. Yes, because the history of celibacy in the sisterhood is just as sordid and seedy as it is in the priesthood. Well, sort of. Historian Jo Ann Kay McNamara is careful to note in her history of nuns that the sisters were never as decadent as the priests: "Some nuns in some houses were incorrigible and some houses were disgraceful, but the great majority of communities at any given moment were free of sexual misconduct."[1] Unlike the priesthood, where a permissive culture of privilege and sexual activity exists, the sisterhood cleaned up its act and changed its thinking completely (long before I arrived on the scene). Strong warnings about sex between sisters were a big part of "sister formation" from day one in the Sisters of the Holy Cross. The message was seriously clear that any sexual activity between sisters (or anyone else) would result in swift and immediate dismissal; there was zero tolerance from day one. They weren't kidding, either. Several suspects were whisked away in the middle of the night, never to be spoken of or heard from again. We knew they were gone for good when their napkin rings disappeared from the breakfast table. That's the only way we knew someone got sent home; and that's how nuns used to shun, with a whole other kind of silence. I suspect some still do.

We could also be dismissed immediately for being in one another's cells (bedrooms) at any time, or if we grew too attached to a particular friend, more commonly referred to as PFs. Not even the appearance of impropriety was tolerated. Disinterest was the total name of the nun game and that included one another as well. No best friends allowed. No social coupling. No special attachments because a closeness with one separates us in that way from the rest. Well, we had PFs anyhow. We found soul mates, thank God, and no such separation or sex I know of happened; and it didn't happen, I suspect, because no one I knew wanted it to. That thought wasn't in our minds. No sister I know was ever obsessed with sex or went crazy from lack of it.

That's not to say that sexual activity never occurs in the sisterhood, or that sisters are mysteriously immune to being in love. Both are bound to happen to someone sometime, and in the sisterhood they happen so rarely, so carefully, and so soulfully. Every sister I know who's been there will tell you the same thing. Being in love is never about sex. It's what feels like another God-given call, something equally divine. There's no greater turning point than that in anyone's life, not to mention the life of a nun. Celibacy is a lifetime effort in the sisterhood, as is any loving vow. On occasion it may become necessary to leave it for a while in order to find out more deeply what celibacy is again, what it is we were called to in the beginning, and what it is we're called to now. When sisters fall in love, most find it necessary to take time out. That's how profoundly sexual relationships can shift attention and energy elsewhere. They, too, are full of the loving power of God.

In the sisterhood I've known, it's customary to take leave for a while if we decide to move forward with a sexual relationship, so as *not* to cause scandal (which is why we don't see much of it). The sisters taking leave are more conscious of scandal than anyone else and great care is taken to give not even the appearance of impropriety. Even so, I've never known a sister who, by anyone's standards, is even close to what you'd call sexually active, promiscuous, or deviant. That's why you don't see nuns living double lives or getting arrested picking up girls on street corners. Unless I am completely blind, you will never see in the sisterhood the sexual depravity we see in the priesthood. From day one, sexual relationships in the sisterhood were declared unacceptable, and as far as I know, that zero-tolerance policy hasn't changed one bit.

Even in the 1970s, when sexual activity between newly Vatican II–liberated priests and sisters appeared rampant (especially on university campuses), its impact and consequences were received quite differently by the priesthood and the sisterhood. One sister told a 1970s story of her superior and the pastor literally taking off together in the middle of the night. Everyone was shocked first by the dramatic and scandalous getaway, then again months later when things between them didn't work out as planned. The priest was readmitted to priesthood without much ado, while the sister was shunned by her community (she probably still is today). While both responses seem wrong to me, it's clear that the sisterhood had zero tolerance for their behavior, while the priesthood saw it as no big deal. In the priesthood, sexual activity and regrettable consequences are not uncommon. Nothing affects the ordained ability to be a priest, not even criminally deviant behavior. In the Catholic priesthood, and according to Catholic teaching, a bad priest can still deliver good sacraments, the ultimate privilege. Not so in the sisterhood.

✢ ✢ ✢

Given zero tolerance for sexual activity in the sisterhood, everyone wonders what happens with all the sexual energy. How can sisters stand a virtual lifetime without sex? How come we don't explode (or maybe you know some who have)? Strong external supports are absolutely essential and two of the biggest and strongest are community and service, sisterhood and work. Gertrude Stein understood celibacy perfectly when she wrote, "Sex is a part of something of which the other parts are not sex at all." Two of the other parts for me are also community and service, best friends and creative work. That's where I find sublimated sexual energy made so "sublime," so divine, and so full of everlasting kinds of life.

It's not hard to understand how a celibate life without sisters and soul mates can easily become meaningless and unbearable, and how a celibate life without a commitment to sisterhood can slowly but surely wear down. The only way we can bear the depth of solitude that we embrace in vowing celibacy is in knowing the depths of its sisterhood. As sisters, we are never as alone as we sometimes have every reason to feel. There's always a community of women who are as soulfully solitary as we are, and just as soulfully together. There is no greater comfort to any woman than the divine comfort found in true and lasting sisterhood, both in and out of the convent.

Creative work is the primary divine path that sexual energy in the sisterhood takes to naturally. Not just any work, although it could be just any work, depending on how creatively and lovingly it's done. The most important part of everything we do is how much we love doing it and how much it expands our ability to be more loving and compassionate, more creative and fun to be with. When Gandhi discovered the call to celibacy, his divine insight was similar to that of Gertrude Stein's. Sex isn't just physical energy. More than anything, sex is the energy behind love and creative work. Sacred sexual energy can be channeled anywhere. Sex is one of its manifestations. Writing is another, as is all creative work. In the sisterhood, sexual energy becomes transformed into the creative part of everything we do, part of the prayers, works, joys, and sufferings of our days. That's how much sex is a part of our lives in the sisterhood. And in that way we can't live without it, either.

So prepare yourself now for something entirely different in looking at celibacy in the sisterhood. The vow is treasured, experienced, understood, and lived quite differently by women called to religious life, which is why we do not read in the news about the deviant sexual activity of nuns. It's not happening today because it hasn't been happening for centuries. In looking at the church's priesthood from its beginning, we see a history of celibacy despised, ignored, and lived so consistently wrong. And in looking at the sisterhood from the beginning, what we'll see is an entirely different history. A liberating history of what religious life was like among the Church Mothers, and most important of all, a history of women divinely capable and committed to reforming themselves and changing the misguided thinking of their medieval ways.

In the sisterhood, celibacy has everything to do with being touched by God and called to lives of service, and nothing to do with sexual activity or the lack of it. Among the sisters I know, our celibate lifestyle comes from an extraordinary experience of God, a liberating way of loving, and an independence that frees us to do the work we're called to. That's how much celibacy in the sisterhood has more to do with God and a life of prayer than it ever does a lifestyle with no men or sex. With all due respect to both, we're simply not that interested in either—at least not in the way the rest of the world seems to be. In looking at sisterhood from the beginning, we will see in every age how celibacy emerges as a great liberator of women, inside and out—altogether contrary to how we saw celibacy emerge in the priesthood, as the great oppressor of men, inside and out. The history of the Church Mothers is not that of the Church Fathers, no more than women's experience of life is the same as that of men. It's no surprise, then, that our experience of God and religious life would be equally different, and nowhere is that difference revealed more clearly than in the religious experience of celibacy.

You will never see in the sisterhood the scandal and hypocrisy that are characteristic of the Catholic priesthood. It's simply not happening, and if it was, that silence would eventually be broken. The 40 percent of nuns who have reported sexual abuse have only begun to speak, and all of those silences can't be kept much longer. The power of truth has grown too strong. What we see in the sisterhood, throughout its medieval history, is how scandal among nuns became nonexistent. Slowly but surely, the sisterhood moved toward the zero tolerance it has known for centuries.

Even though today there are only a handful of sisters (as we've known them) left, what's happening in the church will surely transform the sisterhood, just as it's doing to the priesthood. The gods who have been calling women to sisterhood for thousands of years have not lost their voice, and women all over the world, if anything, are just beginning to waken to the divine energy within, to rekindle those sacred fires, and to hear the call of women to sisterhood. Mountains of oppression are beginning to move because we are beginning to see them. The gods have begun to waken all women, and since the very beginning that's all the sisterhood ever needed: a handful of women and Thee.

4

Sisterhood in the Beginning

In the beginning, sisterhood was a religion in itself. "No institution is older than this sisterhood."[1] When goddesses were worshipped (as well as gods), it was the vestal virgins who left home at an early age (some as young as six), cut their hair short, dressed in a white robe, wore an ornamental headband, and promised the Goddess Vesta at least thirty years of virginity. Vesta is one of three Virgin Goddesses who lived on Mount Olympus along with Artemis and Athena. Of this Holy Trinity, Vesta is worshipped as the divine guardian of home and hearth fire, the holy keeper of home fires burning and hearts yearning. It's the Goddess Vesta who first called an order of women into priesthood and sisterhood, first called women into her holy service as vestal virgins, religion's first nuns.

A sacred fire burned in the Temple of Vesta, home of the Goddess, and it was the exclusive job of the vestal virgins to ensure that it continued burning uninterrupted. Living communally within the temple, these virgins were society's keepers of the eternal flame. Their single-hearted work was that of tending its sacred fire day and night, never taking their eyes off the eternal flame within the Temple of the Goddess or within the temple of their own virgin soul. In the same way that Christianity made our souls Temples of the Holy Ghost, in the eyes of the Goddess Vesta our souls were made Temples of the Sacred Fire. That's why in service of the Virgin Goddess the most important work becomes that of keeping soul fires burning and sacred hearts yearning. It's the exclusive work of the vestal virgins to keep the hearts and souls of everyone awake and fired up, so to speak, full of divine life and extraordinary experiences.

So mysteriously and powerfully important was the contemplative work of vestal virgins to the well-being of all Roman society, that sisters would be scourged mercilessly in public, even buried alive if the sacred fire went out during their shift. So powerful is the temple fire for ancients that they believed terrible darkness and destruction would befall Rome if the flame were extinguished, even for a second. The safety and security of Rome lay literally in the celibate service of the vestal virgins. As long as the sacred fire within the temple continued to burn, all manner of things would be well. The contemplative work of these vestal virgins, these very first nuns, is the life or death work of the sisterhood throughout history. Keep the sacred fire burning within our souls and the soul of Holy Mother Church; never allow soul fires to be extinguished. But scourged mercilessly in public by city officials? Buried alive with a little bit of bread and water? What is it about tending the sacred fire that becomes a life or death matter for the poor vestal virgins who nodded off? And why does the fire being extinguished, even for a second, have such dire consequences for the whole Roman Empire? Power doesn't get any more powerful than that, and its divine secret lies in the sacredness of the eternal flame. Quite clearly, this was no ordinary fire. Nothing in the temple was as it appeared. Everything was charged with the presence of gods.

For our ancestors, fire on the altar was a sign that the Goddess was right there with them. And every time a candle or bonfire was lit in religious rituals, those gathered around its flame entered into its divine transforming energy. Alice Sebold writes about that kind of sacred fire in *The Lovely Bones.* The story is told from the afterlife by a fourteen-year-old girl, Susie Salmon, who was brutally raped and murdered in a cornfield. On the first anniversary of her death, she noticed, "In my heaven I buzzed with heat and energy as more and more people reached the cornfield and lit their candles and began to hum a low dirge-like song. . . ." The fires we light in prayer buzz everyone in heaven with heat and energy: That's a powerful way of thinking about fire, a way that goes far beyond what we see — so far beyond that it seems we've lost sight of that kind of sacred fire completely. Somehow between then and now, nearly all the sacred got taken out of fire, the divine buzz of heat and energy seems long gone.

In the Temple of Vesta, the sacred fire is the Goddess's dwelling place. As long as the eternal flame burns, the Goddess is at home with her people. In fire, ancients see the presence of deities. Hebrew Scriptures describe God as "a consuming fire," and God speaks to Moses from a burning bush. But we look at fire and don't think twice about it. To us fire symbolizes nothing other than what it is, and does what we see it do — light a cigarette, warm a room, cook a meal, destroy everything in its path. Most of us see nothing sacred in fire at all (except for firefighters who must see the face of God in every flame). But our ancestors looked at fire and fell to their knees before the deities burning within. No wonder the Romans believed disaster would strike if the eternal flame ever went out. The absence of the Goddess, even for a second, was experienced literally as a matter of life and death. We need to go beyond what we see when we look at fire and note the presence of deities. We need to look that far in order to see how sisterhood was created in the beginning.

The virginity of the Goddess Vesta and that of the women called to her service is unlike anything we know or understand when we think of celibacy. Everyone's first reaction is "no sex," and then comes a joke. Celibacy is mostly made a joke of in our thinking, jokes that usually make me laugh. For example, there's a memorable episode of the 1980s TV sitcom *The Golden Girls* in which Sophia (Dorothy's live-in mother) decides to join the convent at the age of eighty-something. The girls are sitting around the kitchen table eating cheesecake and discussing Sophia's laughable decision. Blanche ("the slut") is the first to speak her mind: "Nun? I can't believe anyone would want to be a nun. I mean the name alone says it all!" Even I jokingly describe the sisterhood as "nun of this and nun of that" and tell everyone who asks that I give up sex for Lent. But joking aside, something totally different is going on here in the virginity of the Goddess. The Goddess Vesta invites women to a divine experience of virginity that has absolutely everything and absolutely nothing to do with sex.

How can that be? How can virginity have everything and nothing to do with sex? If celibacy has nothing to do with sex and not having any, then what is it? A divine mystery, according to Catholic teaching. The virginity of Jesus' Mother Mary has nothing to do with sexual experience, not even marriage and childbirth. Catholics believe that the Virgin Mary (like all Virgin Goddesses) remains ever virgin before, during, and after the birth of Jesus Christ. She is somehow mysteriously able to remain virgin throughout her life, including marriage and childbirth. Mysteries don't get more unfathomable than that.

There is nothing about the virginity of goddesses that is understood literally at all. Regardless of sexual experience and childbirth, virgin souls remain untouched. No matter what happens to their bodies, they remain mysteriously virgin. There is far more to the virginity of the Goddess than meets our eye. But we need to see that far now, way beyond what meets our eye, because therein lies the sacred soul of all Virgin Goddesses (including the Virgin Mary), and therein lies the virgin soul of the sisterhood. Married or not, every woman in every age needs to know how to remain virgin.

The first thing we see if we go beyond what meets our eye is that celibacy makes sense to women in a way it never can to men. One of the divine experiences virginity offered to women in the ancient world (and now) is a lifestyle free from the sexual expectations of men, the sexual demands and abuses of husbands, and the decades-long burden of childbearing. In our world, men are born free of all forms of submissiveness and enjoy the full liberties of the unmarried (married or not). What virginity gave to women in the beginning is the same divine equality celibacy offers to women now, inside and out: the opportunity to experience the fullness of equality and the fullness of life that goes along with it.

In writing about the role of the vestal virgins, Elizabeth Abbott explains how virginity worked to their advantage, both in and out of the temple. Not only did these contemplative women serve the Goddess Vesta exclusively, body and soul, but they also served as the heart and soul of Roman society, looked upon as blessed among women, touched in an extraordinary way by the sacred fire of the Goddess.

> By far the best known of antiquity's virgins were the vestals, in whose perpetual chastity the highest authorities of state and all civil society entrusted the security of Rome. In return for this overwhelming responsibility (of keeping the sacred fires burning), the vestals lived deeply satisfying lives as revered and powerful women of such exalted status that, alone of Roman women, they enjoyed the same legal rights as men.[2]

For women, power doesn't get more divine than that, and enjoying equal rights and opportunities is all it takes. So mysteriously liberating was the experience of virginity for the vestals that even in a patriarchal world—often brutally so—they enjoyed full equality with men, the only women in Rome to do so. No wonder so many of the vestal virgins lived in the temple for life. After thirty years of being treated like a Goddess, what woman in her rightly liberated mind would want to give that up? After all that time, I bet they, too, couldn't imagine living any other way. That's how profoundly life transforming and soul fulfilling God-given celibacy can be. Those who bear the inner light of the sacred fire also discover heaven on earth. In return for keeping the sacred fire burning, the vestal virgins enjoyed the fullness of life.

As above, so below. The esteemed vestal virgins demonstrate what life can be like for women who spend their lives kindling the sacred fires burning within their souls. Their physical virginity matches their spiritual strength. What matters most in the life of these vestal sisters is the virgin soul. What always matters most is the spark of divine life inside all of us that we must never allow anyone to extinguish, most of all ourselves. Of the Goddess Vesta one ancient wrote, "Thou art the pristine spirit, the nature of which is bliss"—heaven on earth, the divine fullness of life here and now, as well as in the eternal life to come. That's what we have to lose when we lose our virgin soul. Bliss.

If we look far beyond what meets our eye, we can feel inside when our light is being extinguished. We feel suffocated, silenced, ignored, bored and boring, sick and tired, even buried alive. When that happens, lives become sadly like all those whose sacred fire has been extinguished along with any hope of happiness. Hopelessness is a sure sign that the eternal flame inside is nearly extinguished. The vestal virgins serve to remind us how essential it is to tend the sacred fires and heart's desires of our own virgin soul, married or not. Above and below, it truly is a matter of life and death.

The virgin soul means the same thing today as it did in the beginning. Those touched by the Goddess Vesta belong to no one but her, and their lives belong to no one but them. Those who possess a virgin soul can be no man's wife, nor do they want a husband. They are complete in themselves, with no need for a counterpart. Unmarried is the sacred state of the virgin soul, the lifestyle of those who belong to no one but the Goddess. She who will not have or be had by anyone. In the eyes of the vestal virgins (and all of Rome) there was none more holy, wise, and free than she, inside and out. The mysterious power of the unmarried is one divine dimension of celibacy that we've long lost sight of. That's one sacred fire that appears all but totally extinguished.

Being unmarried, solitary, and contemplative is only half of the lifestyle of the virgin soul. The real divine power of virginity becomes manifest through the extraordinary way in which these women live. Esteemed by all as representatives and messengers of the Goddess, these vestal virgins sound very much like "The Ideal Wife" described in the Book of Proverbs: "Men entrust their hearts to her because she brings them good and not evil all the days of her life. . . . She enjoys the success of her dealings; and at night her lamp is undimmed. . . . She opens her mouth in wisdom and on her tongue is kindly counsel. . . . She is clothed with strength and dignity, and she laughs at the days to come" (31:10–31). Those who bear divinity in their own right are led naturally toward lifestyles of extraordinary dedication and service. That much is clear within the sisterhood of the vestal virgins.

Those who bear divinity in their own right tend not to be submissive to any voice of authority other than that of the Goddess. For example, because virgins tend only to the voice of gods, they need not seek approval from others. Anyone who lives their life in order to please others, be accepted, gain power, or win another's interest or love, is no virgin. We become ever virgin only through living our lives according to the voice of God, the presence of the Goddess in our soul's sacred fires. It's in following single-heartedly our holy intuitions and our sacred heart's desires that we become ever virgin, full of creative and compassionate powers this world cannot survive without. That was true in the beginning with the sisterhood of the vestal virgins. The safety and security of Roman society was entrusted to them completely. They were the makers and keepers of peace on earth.

While the vestal virgins flourished for hundreds of years after the birth of Christ, they, too, were eventually condemned as evil by Christianity in the fourth century along with other pagan cults, and all because of sex. For thousands of years sexual union was revered as the greatest and most sacred rite between the deities and us. Sexual customs, such as fertility rites, became integrated naturally into religious rituals. They were the most sacred expression of human contact with God. Ancient religions believed that whenever a deep abiding love exists, the Goddess becomes fully present in many ways, sexual union being one of them. In the religion of the Goddess, there is nothing in us that is not divine. But not so with the religion of Christianity whose Crusade it became to condemn the sanctity of sex as evil, and whose mission it became to extinguish the sacred fire of the Goddess, above and below, once and for all.

In condemning sexual pleasure as evil, Christianity condemns all virgin priestesses as prostitutes and sorcerers, hunting them down, destroying their temples, and publicly torturing them to death, doing all in their priestly power to destroy the sanctity of sexual union as the heart and soul of religion. Along with the virgin priestesses went the goddesses to whom they vowed their lives. The sacred fires of sex are condemned as evil by the Church Fathers, and their primary job is to see that those eternal flames remain extinguished, especially in women, whom they blame for starting them. While Christianity wholeheartedly endorses and honors as holy the virgin's sacred liberty to refuse sex forever, it does all in its power to condemn as evil the virgin's freedom to accept sacred sex as well. Quite clearly, that's not the kind of virginity the Church Fathers had in mind. To the literal-minded, virginity can't be both. It's impossible. To a mind obsessed with sex, uncontrolled virginity becomes just as dangerous as uncontrolled sexuality.

The virgin soul can literally mean only one thing in Christianity: no sex. The only way women can be seen as holy, as equal, as anything other than a sex object, is if they vow never to have sex, never to be a sexual object, and never act like the evil, lustful seducers of men that we are. The desexualized, neutered woman (like the castrated man) becomes the New Virgin in Christianity. She who denies sex forever and becomes a "Bride of Christ." She who extinguishes the sacred fire within her soul once and for all. She who vows and allows her heart's desire to remain hidden, silent, and buried alive. That's the New Virgin the Church Fathers literally carved out; or so they thought. Yet sex is one sacred fire they can't extinguish in themselves, much less in anyone else, especially women.

Just as the vestal virgins emerged as antiquity's first nuns, so, too, do the women of Galilee who followed Jesus emerge as Christianity's first nuns. And it's not unlikely that these two groups of women would've known each other and shared sisterhood. Vestal virgins naturally would have been drawn to the Jesus Movement, given its wide reputation for liberating women and the oppressed, for rekindling the sacred fires of those whose soulful flames are dying. And both groups of women experienced profoundly how their hearts burned when their God spoke, and how their lives changed miraculously when they followed the divine voice.

In the beginning, Christianity was viewed widely as a religion of the oppressed, and in every age that category automatically includes an overwhelming majority of women. Given centuries of female-dominated house churches, it's entirely likely that vestal virgins served as hosts or guest presiders of Christian "table communities." In the Jesus Movement, the vestals would have felt at home and been treated as the goddesses they were. Some merging of virgin sisterhoods appears to happen in Christianity (at least in spirit), because the women who follow Jesus seem to possess the same virgin soul as their vestal sisters and seem to hear the same sacred call to sisterhood.

In the same divine spirit of the Goddess Vesta, Jesus calls disciples to break family ties and follow. Family expectations, even society's norms, mean nothing in the Jesus Movement. All that matters is hearing the Word of God and keeping it, listening to the deities in our hearts and souls and keeping the sacred fires burning. The Jesus Movement was so attractive to women and the oppressed because its message set them free. Like the Goddess Vesta, so, too, does Jesus call us to break out of the life that suffocates us and set ourselves free. And so deeply do women hear that divine call that they, too, drop everything and follow. They, too, become virgin in following Christ, and they, too, cannot go back to living any other way.

Just as celibacy freed vestal virgins from the endless burden of abusive men and endless childbearing, so, too, does virginity become the magic key to a priestly life for women in the early church. In refusing to marry (or remarry), women step outside of every sexist expectation in the service of God, thereby gaining the freedom necessary to minister, preach, and live apostolic lives, ordained or not. Sent out in two's, women and men traveled together in celibate partnership, manifesting not only a new vision of God as love, but also a divine vision of a new social order in which men and women live and work in full and equal partnership. In Christianity, virginity continues to endow women with the divine power of independence normally restricted for men alone. For biblical women, celibacy was experienced as "a good thing."

At the core of the early Christian church, it appeared as though a celibate sisterhood emerged freely and gladly long before a celibate priesthood did by force. Widows, liberated prostitutes, separated wives, virgins, and freed slaves were among those most likely moved by Christ to form a sisterhood of prayer and apostolic service. Virginity continues to wipe out gender differences in those who follow Christ, giving women the divine authority and independence to pursue apostolic lives. Just as perpetual virginity did for vestal virgins in the beginning, so, too, did celibacy remain the divine equalizer for women in the early church. For all intents and purposes, virginity becomes the "free pass" for women into the "boys club," in the name and service of God.

Even as women began to be squeezed out of priestly activities by the Church Fathers, the sisterhood of Church Mothers worked to develop alternative ministries rooted in the Spirit of Christ. It's the sisterhood that developed and built ministries of prayer, prophecy, healing, and counsel and the sisterhood that developed and built communities centered on lives of charity, works of mercy, and fellowship around the table. Just as it did in the beginning, virginity serves as a divine source of power for women in the early church. And the sisterhood of women, called to leave everything and follow Christ, became an equally powerful influence in Christianity, especially among widows.

Widows emerged as a particularly powerful group within the sisterhood of the Jesus Movement. In the New Testament, widows were especially loved and protected by God, and therefore held in high esteem. These women who chose not to remarry become a spiritual ideal in Christianity, completely open in their newly unmarried state to the influence of God and the freedom to do works of charity. Alone as they were after the deaths of their husbands, and many of them wealthy with their inherited estates, it's not surprising that widows organized themselves into sisterhoods and gave their lives to liberating the oppressed. Ever mother and ever virgin became the new Christian ideal for widows: women who gave their unmarried lives forever to prayer, virginity, and charity.

In the New Testament, Peter is written about as having organized three "orders" of widows—two communities devoted to prayer, prophecy, and counsel, while the third cared for sick and poor women. Many wealthy widows who had no intention of marrying again discovered new and liberating lives in the Jesus Movement. Most funded the building of new Christian communities, and most house churches were sponsored and supported by wealthy widows. Quite clearly, women did not join the sisterhood in Christianity to withdraw and escape from the world. That was their old life. That's the life they lived before being liberated by Christ.

On the contrary, celibacy freed widows completely, just as it did the vestal virgins, to restore the heart and soul of society's oppressed, to keep all our sacred fires burning. So much so that by the power of these three orders of widows, all kinds of celibate sisterhoods emerged in the early church, including communities of virgins, hermits, and contemplative nuns. While the women of Galilee became Christianity's first nuns, the sisterhood of widows emerges as the first order of nuns in the church, Christianity's first unordained women priests.

Given the freedom and independence generated naturally within the sisterhood, the church continued to do everything in its power to make sure that women never transcended fully their submissiveness through the virginity movement. In liberating women from the traditional roles of wife and mother, celibacy became for women a divine way to pursue unorthodox lives, always a major source of concern, worry, even alarm for the church. Holy disobedience is what the Church Fathers fear most in their consecrated virgins. Women who don't accept their voice as God's must be silenced and forced to submit, forced to give at least the appearance of holy obedience; forced at least to act as though they're not listening to any other divine voice than that of their ultimate religious superiors, the Church Fathers.

Because virgins were never known in the ancient world as silent or submissive women, any trace of insubordination, any spark of new life reminiscent of their evil pagan past and the full force of church authority, is brought down upon them. Control of its virgins became an ongoing Crusade of the Church Fathers; only with the women, it was not control of their sexually active bodies that was the problem, it was control of their divinely inspired, holy, disobedient souls—that's the problem with women and for women in the sisterhood. Disobedience is a sure sign that the virgins are listening to some other divine voice, a clear sign that the sacred fire within them has not yet been extinguished. The Goddess is still at home. That meant only one thing to Church Fathers: The Church Mothers and their sisters must be forced to submit, body and soul.

Stripping virginity of its sacred transforming powers received its crowning blow theologically when the Church Fathers baptized the sisters' virgin souls with their new role as "Brides of Christ," only not in a loving, mystical sense. Once freed in virginity from all sexual stereotyping, women now became "brides" and not "virgins" of Christ, divinely submissive in the eyes of God and the laws of the church, divinely independent no more. As brides of Christ, the church's virgins became subject to the control of "Christ" on earth, meaning the male priesthood acting *in persona Christi*. All sanctity in the sisterhood was invested in holy obedience to the laws of the church and the teachings of its fathers. Canon laws still regulate the lives of nuns today, and the Vatican demand for holy obedience still attempts to govern the virgin souls in all of its orders of sisterhood, attempts to bind its sisters in "holy silence."

Because celibacy is chosen freely and gladly in the sisterhood, it never was and never will be the problem that it is in the priesthood. Holy obedience became the soulful problem of the Church Mothers, making sure that the divine voice these virgins are obeying comes from the "right God," meaning that of the Church Fathers. While control of the virgin sisterhood, legally and theologically, appeared early in the church's history, I don't see that it ever worked. Not in the beginning, and most certainly not in the Middle Ages. There are sacred fires burning within the souls of virgins that can never be extinguished. That's been true since the very beginning, and continues to be true as we look at sisterhood in the Middle Ages.

5

Sisterhood in the Middle Ages

THE GROWTH OF SISTERHOOD in the Middle Ages, particularly in the twelfth century, is seen as absolutely remarkable by historians, all commenting on the large numbers of women who entered religious life then. While part of the growth would have been proportionate to the general increase in population at that time, something else was going on. Convents couldn't open up fast enough to keep up with demand, and when they did, they were never big enough. In writing about the order of Clarisses, or Poor Clares, Jo Ann Kay McNamara notes,

> By 1400, there were about 400 houses. 250 in Italy, and most of the rest in Spain and France, with a few scattered in England, Germany and eastern Europe. One or two houses may have held more than 200 women but most ran between 50 and 80. In all, probably 15,000 women belonged to the order.[1]

Those numbers are astounding, and not just by today's standards. I don't think the sisterhood has seen anything like it since; which is not to say that it can't happen again.

In order to understand the rapid growth of sisterhood in the Middle Ages, it's important to know what other life choices there were for women at that time. For example, girls were destined for "marriage" at the age of twelve, an arrangement that was more of a real estate deal than anything else. The girl went along with the property the man inherited in marriage. Love and companionship for men seemed to happen outside marriage with mistresses and courtly lovers. If it was true love that the medieval woman wanted in life, she would not have looked for, or expected to find it, in marriage. Obviously the medieval man didn't, either.

Unlike The Ideal Wife revealed in the Book of Proverbs, The Ideal Medieval Wife presents a different portrait. She is submissive to her husband, obeys every request without question, manages the perfect household, cooks a well-balanced meal, and raises as many ideal children as her body can bear, preferably boys. If you've seen the movie *The Stepford Wives,* that's the contemporary image that comes to mind, women modeled by men whose sacred fire is extinguished in marriage. Marriage, childbearing, and a lifetime of submissiveness are what the medieval world expected of its women, as did the Catholic Church. I don't believe that's changed very much, either.

Not only was there an emotional climate of zero tolerance for questioning male authority, but disobedient wives and children were routinely beaten into submission. In the early Middle Ages, wife beating for insubordination was sanctioned by the Catholic Church in its Canon Laws, but its practice was legalized worldwide long before then, and still is in many places of the world. In Africa, for example, women (not men) are still stoned to death for adultery. Like children, slaves, and animals, women were to be controlled, and if necessary, beaten into submission. Violence remained the method of choice in the church for maintaining control and resolving disputes, and physical abuse was accepted widely in Christian households.

As recently as 1913, the Catholic Church sanctioned wife beating in Canon Law, specifying the rod couldn't be thicker than your finger and you couldn't draw blood. The Book of Deuteronomy also advocates beating wives into submission, if necessary. In patriarchy, it's a man's sacred marital duty to head the household and maintain control of his family, using force if necessary. Each one of those beaten women are holy virgins and martyrs we'll never know. And that kind of married martyrdom was not something women dreamed of in the Middle Ages. Marriage was nowhere near the safe and sacred life for medieval women that it can be today.

No thinking woman would choose to be married given those circumstances, and no loving parent would subject their daughter to a lifetime of cruelty and abuse. McNamara estimates that in the tenth and eleventh centuries, "anywhere from a quarter to a third" of the women in convents were widows or married.[2] Avoiding medieval marriage became a very compelling alternative for women in the Middle Ages, many of whom got themselves into the nunnery for a good education (and a life of prayer and service) and many of whom got sent there against their will. Nowadays "Get thee to a nunnery!" is no longer a life sentence for any unwilling woman and religious communities are no longer dumping grounds for society's misfits or the wild daughters of overprotective fathers. The Dark Ages were, indeed, dark in the sisterhood, and nowhere is that clearer than in the medieval nunneries.

In the sixteenth century, half of the rich daughters in Italy were locked up in convents, some as young as three years old. Medieval nunneries were little more than virgin safe houses, virtual prisons with escapees often beaten by nuns and locked up in solitary confinement for years. Many were victims of sexual abuse by nuns and one another. Sexual sinners were sent by priests to the convents for rehab, and the deformed, disabled, and dissolute were sent there for safekeeping (and slave labor). It's no wonder all hell broke loose in the medieval nunneries. They were full of women who never wanted to be there and who hated every day that they were. In that regard, no God was there. Life became literally hell on earth for unwilling nuns and their unwilling victims.

According to Elizabeth Abbott, the nunneries in Italy (like its papacy and priesthood) appear to have been the worst.[3] In Venice, fifteen nunneries were known as public bordellos. Some nuns in convents "had servants, ate lavish meals, and carried pet lap dogs." They also received male callers regularly and maintained rather sophisticated, sexually active lifestyles. Italian nunneries often earned the reputation of being little more than high-class whorehouses with wealthy playboys among their most frequent patrons. And where there were double monasteries—monks' and nuns' residences connected by underground tunnels—there were notoriously nasty habits between the two. Abbott notes, "Bishops routinely issued edicts barring the free intercourse—in all senses—between the male and female sides."

Babies were routinely conceived and born in the abbey, with one English abbess giving birth to a whole convent of kids, twelve to be exact. The worst excesses were in Venice, where nuns and priests engaged freely in public sex, as well as privately in one another's cells (bedrooms). In the fourteenth century, thirty-three brothel-like convents were sued for sexual abuse and prostitution:

> The Benedictine Saint' Angelo di Contorta convent was the most outrageous, though its nuns were drawn from the Venetian elite. The nuns, and two abbesses, did not even bother with discretion but enjoyed sex at picnics and—putting Madre Marcela's vaunted solitude to a more mundane use—in their cells. Babies were conceived and born, lovers quarreled, and jealousy abounded. The pope shut down Saint' Angelo in

1474, but it was just one of many egregiously misbehaving religious institutions.[4]

Throughout history, nuns act just as priests do when celibacy is forced upon them. Once again, it's the old divine law of human nature: The more sex feels prohibited, the more it just goes underground and flourishes so much that it is eventually forced aboveground as well. Everybody acts that way when celibacy is forced upon them. It twists their souls, demonizes their God, and drives them crazy. That kind of craziness became rampant in the medieval sisterhood, and in that regard, the church's nunneries became a clear reflection of its priesthood. They were full of women called by everyone and everything but God. But even at their very worst, nuns were nowhere near as corrupt as the priests. For example, "between 1430 and 1450, 12 out of 220 nuns in Lincoln were found guilty of immoral behavior. In 1514, a general visitation in Norwich found one nun of Crabhouse who had gone wrong out of 8 houses with 72 nuns."[5] As McNamara notes, "Criticism went hand in hand with correction." The sisterhood never accepted sexual permissiveness as part of their religious life.

✝ ✝ ✝

In the world of work there was also little soulful solace or satisfaction to be found by women. Married or not, most women worked because they had to (men were fighting or killed in wars and crusades), and there were few jobs that women didn't do. Yet even though medieval women excelled in the arts, crafts, and business; ran most taverns and inns; administered most charitable services; even led religious and political movements, never did they receive the authority commensurate with their skills, knowledge, experience, and expertise. And never did they earn the right to govern their own guilds and professions. The exercise of authority by women (over men) was cognitively dissonant, altogether unthinkable, to the medieval mind, in the same way that women priests still cannot be imagined by some minds today. The exercise of authority, especially religious authority, is "naturally" unfeminine. By nature, women are weak and emotional, incapable of rational thought and divine insight, and therefore incapable of governing themselves, much less anyone else, especially men. . . .

Only widows became entitled to self-governing privileges. In the Middle Ages they were legion, creating a powerful source of medieval sisterhood just as they did in the early church. All other women remained, in every aspect of life, submissive and subordinate to male authority. Even the most incompetent of the male species was held in greater esteem than the most brilliant medieval woman. And in the world of work, a woman's contribution was valued at half as much as her male counterpart's—paid half as much because it was literally assumed that women ate half as much. That was the basis for job discrimination in the Middle Ages. For as laughable as that may seem, it is not that different today in many parts of the world. That's how much sexist thinking refuses to change. Even the world of work was not a very liberating or fulfilling life choice for medieval women. Most were treated slightly better than slaves in the workplace.

Given the grim choices of marriage and work, and the church's condemnation of women as weak, lustful, and evil, it's no wonder so many looked for safety and salvation in religious life and sisterhood. And no wonder so many nuns went crazy mortifying, abusing, and neglecting their sinful bodies. Even though the monks and Church Fathers grew more hostile over having to support the growth of nunneries throughout Europe, medieval women continued to be drawn to the contemplative life (keeping the sacred fires burning), continued to be liberated and inspired by the gospel of love, and continued to do so in increasingly large numbers. With nothing but discouragement from the Church Fathers, the medieval women's movement into religious life grew to form numerous cloistered communities and uncloistered sisterhoods as well. According to McNamara, "Nothing could stem the tide of vocations or family strategies that filled established houses to the bursting point and caused new, informal foundations to burgeon everywhere."[6]

✢ ✢ ✢

Cloistered life in the nunnery was not the only choice of sisterhood for women called to religious life in the Middle Ages. Also of growing concern and dismay to the Church Fathers were the newly organized (and unorganized) groups of women committed to living a Christian life in celibate sisterhood, only without the constraints of monastic enclosure. Just as cloistered life within the nunnery experienced rapid growth in the Middle Ages, so too did uncloistered sisterhood emerge as a powerful alternative for medieval women drawn to religious sisterhood but not in the nunnery. The most popular and influential of these "secular" sisterhoods was that of the Beguines, a twelfth-century women's movement born in Belgium, ignored by historians because they didn't live as "real nuns," but of utmost importance here in looking at how medieval women sought religious sisterhood, both in and out of the convent.

Given the chaos and corruption that filled the nunneries and surrounded the Church Fathers in the Middle Ages, it's no wonder women drawn to apostolic lives of prayer and service would seek an alternative like that of the Beguines. Single, married, or widowed, the Beguines lived as nuns outside the convent, and according to the rule of life each community decided upon as its own. While living as a Beguine, all vow informally to remain celibate as well as free to marry or enter the nunnery. Celibacy, simplicity, and charitable works governed their lives, as did a single-hearted devotion to prayer, study, and teaching. And just as we find among their cloistered sisters, so too do we find within the Beguine sisterhood the emergence of numerous visionaries and mystics. In and out of the convent, the sisterhood in the Middle Ages endowed us with the richest mystical writings to date, all of which eventually became spiritual ammo for the Church Fathers and their Inquisitions.

Everything about the Beguines irritated the Church Fathers from the very start, especially their independence from all authority, male or female. Neither husband, nor priest, nor parent could control these women, and furthermore, these women had no desire to control one another. Even though there were thousands of Beguines throughout Europe, never did they organize themselves into a "religious order" with superiors, motherhouses, rules, and constitutions. The Beguines hold nothing in common other than a celibate commitment to prayer and apostolic service, and no woman is superior or submissive; all are treated equal. All are one. In obedience to the spirit of God in one another, the voice of each sister is revered as holy, and in communion with one another decisions are made. The only "order" and "rule" within the Beguine sisterhood is that which each community accepts freely and lovingly as its own.

Within the Beguine sisterhood the sacred fire of virgin independence was revered as its eternal flame. All sisters were self-supporting, tax paying, even property owning and sharing. Some Beguines chose to live at home and care for family, while others moved in together and many lived alone. Just as in the Jesus Movement, many medieval women, especially widows, shared financial resources with sisters in need, even willing homes and property to other Beguines. Because poverty was epidemic among women in the Middle Ages (as it is now), most communities chose a cooperative lifestyle and pooled resources, and all tended to congregate and settle in the heart of cities, often near hospitals, churches, or other religious communities. The groups of Beguines that came to settle all over Europe by the fifteenth century became known as Beguinages, meaning a sisterhood or community of Beguines.

Free from monastic enclosure and church control, all Beguinages were self-governing, living according to their own agreed-upon rule. At first, Beguines dressed like most medieval women, only more plainly and in darker colors. Later they developed a simple blue or gray habit, nothing extravagant or ornamental and nothing difficult to care for or assemble. The habit of Beguines came to symbolize their lifestyle as religious women, plain and simple. Contemplative life as a Beguine also included spiritual exercises common to their cloistered sisters and very similar to those we observed in 1964: daily mass, praying the Divine Office, special community prayers and meditations, examinations of conscience, spiritual reading, and retreats. Some communities chose more contemplative lifestyles than others depending upon the solitary needs of the sisters, but all shared a profound call to lives of prayer, and did so, in the words of Rilke's poem "The Beguinage," "in order that they may better understand why there should be such love in them."

I imagine the lifestyle adopted by each Beguinage would attract women who shared a vision of contemplative and apostolic life. All Beguines treasured as a divine rule the freedom to choose their own communities, living conditions, and ministries. And all shared the ministry of hospitality to those in need. The informal vow of poverty in the Beguinage fulfilled itself through sisterly hospitality, the open offer of shelter to travelers and the homeless, free care of the sick, and a sisterly table community to all in need. Would that we all vowed informally that kind of poverty and offered that kind of sisterly hospitality.

In the mind of many medieval women, there was no lifestyle more divinely free than that of the Beguine sisterhood. The life of every Beguine is freely chosen, with none of the forced submissiveness or deprivation upon which medieval marriage and the nunnery were built. Theirs was a sisterhood called to live smack dab in the middle of the world, not hidden forever in the cloister, a vision of sisterhood unlike anything the world had seen since the Jesus Movement in the early church. Poverty, celibacy, and obedience found expression within the Beguines in an entirely different way, solemnly lived instead of solemnly vowed. Of these extremely popular and powerful street sisters, one supportive sixteenth-century bishop in Antwerp wrote:

> . . . it was a common capacity of many pious women in Belgium to rejoice in excellence rather than promise it. They preferred to remain chaste perpetually than to vow perpetual chastity. Likewise they were more eager to obey than to vow obedience, to cultivate poverty by frugal use of their fortunes than to abandon everything at once: they might be the kinder to the poor if something were left. They preferred to submit daily, as it were, to obedience within the enclosure than to be confined once and for all. In constant spontaneity they found compensation for perpetual claustration.[7]

No wonder medieval women flocked to the Beguines. A thirteenth-century English monk reported, "They have so multiplied within a short time that 2000 have been reported in Cologne and the neighboring cities."[8] Given the oppressive lifestyle of marriage, work, and even the nunnery, women needed no encouragement in seeing how divinely liberating the Beguine sisterhood was—soulfully reminiscent of the Jesus Movement, even the vestal virgins they may have remembered. Neither wives, nor lovers, nor nuns, the Beguine sisterhood appeared as heaven on earth to thousands of medieval women, the most divinely appealing lifestyle of all. Despite their lack of a common order, and despite the fact that they never were and never wanted to be "real nuns" as governed by the Church Fathers, the Beguines emerged in the Middle Ages, as they do in my eyes now, as one of sisterhood's most powerful and prophetic movements: divinely powerful for thousands of medieval women, and divinely prophetic today, a sign of sisterhood to come.

While the Beguines were recognized widely and esteemed highly throughout Europe as semimystical sisterhoods, their free spirits and unregulated lives never received anything but suspicion and disapproval from ecclesiastical authorities. No big surprise there. The independence of the Beguines from church control and supervision were a huge source of irritation for the Church Fathers. An independent, self-governing community of religious women was unheard of in the Middle Ages, and the Church Fathers were quick in their response to ensure that it stayed that way. The Beguines were nothing but trouble in the medieval church from the start, refusing to be supervised by anyone, especially the Church Fathers. The fact that they lasted as long and as successfully as they did is nothing short of one big medieval miracle.

Essential to the Beguine charism is preserving as sacred fire the celibate independence and uncloistered manner of their apostolic life, both of which were anathema in the medieval eyes of God and the Catholic Church. All the saintly success and widespread popularity earned the Beguines ecclesiastical harassment and hatred. And given what we know of priesthood in the Middle Ages, it's not surprising to learn that the Church Fathers looked at the Beguine sisterhood and saw a thinly disguised women's liberation movement designed to escape all male authority—in marriage and in the church—making it the most subversively evil women's movement of all. The Church Fathers looked at the Beguines and saw nothing but a kind of holy anarchy they could not tolerate.

Akin to the Beguines in their religious independence were the numerous hermits, recluses, and "anchorites" who populated the cities and countryside throughout Europe. These were women in the Middle Ages called to live the contemplative life in solitude, not in the nunnery and not in community. Of all medieval women called to contemplative life, there were and always will be those whose need for solitude demands that they live alone and devote their lives solely to contemplative works. In wanting to live a solitary religious life, many medieval women chose to live in hermitages and have contact with no one, or only those who come seeking spiritual direction. And while some of these solitary sisters were affiliated with and supported by monastic communities, all maintained independence from church control. All lived solitary lives according to the rule that best served their contemplative needs.

Common among the medieval lifestyles of these solitary sisters was that of the anchorites like Julian of Norwich. These are women whose hermitage was built adjacent to, or "anchored" to, the church. In the Church of Saint Julian of Norwich, for example, her cell is built on the south wall of the church, with an inside window from which she attended mass and received communion and an outside window opening out into the churchyard.

At this window, Julian received and spoke with visitors who came for spiritual direction. The cell, which can still be entered today, has been made into a side chapel, with her desk now a memorial altar, upon which stands an engraved stone that reads:

Here Dwelt Mother Julian
Anchoress of Norwich
c. 1342–1430
"Thou art enough to me."

It was there that Julian experienced and wrote her one and only book, *Revelations of Divine Love*. Among the solitary sisterhood in the Middle Ages, many women, like Julian, chose to live in solitude as anchorites.

As the Church Fathers became increasingly disturbed over the growth of these free-spirited religious communities and recluses in every major European city, so, too, did their coercive efforts to put the "nun" back into sisterhood, to control once and for all those independent, uncontrollable religious women. Not knowing what else to do with the Beguines who were neither nuns nor wives, and unable to bear such free-spirited religious sisterhoods, the church in the twelfth century began to officially condemn all women who called themselves religious without submitting to monastic rule. And when that didn't really work, they ordered with church laws all religious women back into the cloister and back under church control. The Lateran Council of 1139 prohibited any new religious rules or orders without papal approval. No religious women could live unsupervised.

Unable to bear the "anarchy" of the Beguines and recluses any longer, popes in the thirteenth and fourteenth centuries reinforced the Lateran Council by issuing a series of what are fittingly called papal bulls, making it Canon Law for all religious women everywhere to live in a cloister. The full force of the Catholic Church emerged as papal bull to eliminate all forms of sisterhood beyond their control. There could be no such thing as a celibate "free spirit" in the lust-filled eyes of the fathers. The only way women, like men, could ever live celibate lives is when they were locked up forever in the cloister, forever under church control, or so they continued to lead everyone to believe. In condemning the Beguines as an "abominable sect," the Church Fathers proclaimed:

> We have been told that certain women commonly called Beguines, afflicted by a kind of madness, discuss the Holy Trinity and the divine essence and express opinions on matters of faith and sacraments contrary to the catholic faith, deceiving many simple people. Since these women promise no obedience to anyone and do not renounce their property or profess an approved Rule, they are certainly not religious; although they wear a habit and are associated with such religious orders as they find congenial. . . . We have therefore decided and decreed with the approval of the Council that the Beguine way of life is to be permanently forbidden and altogether excluded from the Church of God.[9]

In the eyes of the Church Fathers, the most dangerous part of the Beguines was found in their spiritual independence—in their mysticism, in their mystical beliefs, writings, and teachings. Above all, the Beguines were known to be contemplative women of prayer, many of whom were sought out widely as visionaries, prophets, and spiritual advisers. Through their writings the

Beguine mystics quickly became well known and loved throughout Europe, and it's those writings that the Church Fathers condemned as heresy. Any claim to divine authority other than that of the Church Fathers has always been condemned as heresy, and most mystic's writings have been condemned as such by the church in their day. Why? Because the truths mystics reveal tend to dismiss church rules as unnecessary, even contrary to the voice of God.

After his dark night of the soul, the sixteenth-century Spanish mystic John of the Cross concluded that love is the one and only answer to everything: loving God, loving neighbor, loving life, and loving ourselves. Having seen the divine light at the end of the dark night, "Love and do what you will" is what John of the Cross advises. The message hidden in all dark nights is found in the gospel of love. I bet the Church Fathers were none too pleased to hear that being preached to the "simple people" in the pew. God forbid the faithful from loving God and doing what they will. Julian of Norwich not only reveals in her *Showings* (meaning "revelations") a God who is Mother, but also concludes that "Sin is no blame, but worship;" a sure-fire double barreled shockaroo for church teaching.[10] Anyone who experiences sin as worship is guaranteed to be condemned by the church in every age, and referring to God as Mother is still a papal no-no. Mystics and their free-spirited divine messages were nothing but clear heretical targets for the Inquisition, and the Beguines were no exception. They were marked for extinction in the eyes of the Church Fathers from the start.

One of the mystic martyrs of the Beguine sisterhood is Marguerite Porete, a fourteenth-century Belgian mystic best known for her controversial and condemned writings in *A Mirror for Simple Souls*.[11] Marguerite was condemned for heresy and burned at the stake for ideas about the "free spirit" all souls enter in union with God, the free spirit as a holy spirit free of all rules and control, including those of the Catholic Church. In explaining how liberated the soul becomes in union with God, Marguerite writes.

> The soul at the highest stage of her perfection and nearest the dark night is beyond noticing the rules of the Church. She is commanded by pure love, which is a higher mistress than what we call "charitable works." She has surpassed so far beyond the works of virtue that she no longer knows what they are about—but yet she has assimilated them to the point where they are part of her, the Church cannot control her—[12]

In a nutshell, that's why the Inquisition burned to death Marguerite Porete and her sisters. The church could not control them. That's why the Church Fathers condemned as heretics all Beguines and anchorites who would not submit to their "divine" authority. We can only imagine how liberating and inspiring those words were to the thousands of Beguines who resisted church control. And how devastated they must have been to have so many of their sisters burned at the stake for the "free-spirited" heretical beliefs they shared. These saintly women who promised obedience to no one but God barely survived the Middle Ages, and only a handful exist in Europe today. Even so, I have a feeling their day will come soon. Out of all the powerful sisterhoods that emerged in the Middle Ages, both in and out of the cloister, I see the Beguines as holding the greatest hope for the future of religious sisterhood, as well as sisterhood now.

6

Sisterhood Now

BY THE TIME WOMEN'S religious orders were founded in the United States, they were already totally different from medieval nunneries. Thanks to the Holy Spirit of the Reformation and some divinely inspired women, miracles were worked in cleaning up all the medieval corruption in the sisterhood—most important of all, the admission requirements. By the mid-nineteenth century, convents were already filled with women who truly felt called by God to religious life and celibate sisterhood. The days of turning the nunnery into a death sentence for misguided girls were over. Undesirables need not apply. Few girls joined the convent because they were forced to, and even if they did, most didn't last long. Those not truly called by God to sisterhood either couldn't stand it and left, became sick and got sent home, or were dismissed against their will. Unwilling nuns, as well as unhealthy and scandalous behavior, were no longer acceptable in the sisterhood. At the dawn of the second millennium, nuns in this country emerged completely transformed, finally becoming, once again, the holy and apostolic women they were called to be in the beginning.

In every way it seems as though the sisterhood was reborn at the dawn of the twentieth century, very much in the contemplative spirit of their cloistered sisters and equally in the apostolic spirit of the Beguine sisterhood. Those brave and visionary women who founded the religious orders we have today were both educated and dedicated, saint and businesswoman, cloistered and uncloistered. Nearly a third of women's colleges in the United States were founded by nuns at that time. It was then also that the sisterhood became a powerful workforce in Catholic health care and education, not to mention the backbone of parish life. The women who gave birth to the religious sisterhood we know now were a new breed of nun in their day. Once again the Church Mothers emerge strongly as holy and apostolic, just as they did in the Jesus Movement.

For as independent and as visionary as the founding sisters of religious orders were, so, too, were they governed and controlled by the Church Fathers, local and papal. By the nineteenth century, church control of all nuns was a foregone conclusion. Rome refused to recognize or support any sisters who didn't live in a convent with a superior, wear a habit, and abide by its canon laws. In the Catholic Church, no one is self-governing except the Church Fathers, least of all the Church Mothers (even to the point of the nineteenth-century papal prohibition forbidding hospital sisters from working in obstetric units or nurseries, believing such intimate contact would be harmful to a nun's chastity).[1] That's how obsessively involved Church Fathers became in regulating every aspect of nun's lives, and that's how obsessed they were with sex.

Even in my day, and for the very same reason, we weren't allowed to hold children or babies, nor could we sit next to men in public (including family). All kinds of church rules came down to govern nun's lives, most of which reflect nothing other than the Church Fathers' literal and sex-obsessed understanding of celibacy. They saw sex everywhere, even in hospital nurseries. For as smart and as visionary as nuns were in building the American sisterhood, that's the kind of "divine" authority that governed much of their lives; and whatever Father said, Sister did.

The whole way women's religious orders grew and developed in the United States is the result of church governance and guidelines, including the authority structure of superiors and subordinates, rules of order, and the establishment of motherhouses. All communities of Catholic sisters were required to establish motherhouses, a single geographical location (usually where they were founded), where all members "grow up," so to speak, and become full-fledged nuns. For example, the Sisters of the Holy Cross have their motherhouse in Notre Dame, Indiana, on the same grounds as Saint Mary's College, the women's school they founded in 1844. That's where we went for our "sister formation," and that's where we went for our college education. The college became the Mother of our Mind, and the motherhouse became the Mother of our Soul. Throughout a sister's life, she is called to return to the motherhouse for spiritual renewal, continuing education, community meetings, sister reunions, and community celebrations. Those communities of visionary women who organized into religious orders were required by church law to establish motherhouses, which happened to serve well the sisterhood's growing needs.

The motherhouse grew to function as the sister's general headquarters, as well as its training grounds. Usually, the community's highest-ranking members live and work in the motherhouse, as do the sisters who manage the convent's administrative and support services, like the kitchen, laundry, and convent infirmary. I thought it was called motherhouse because that's where the Church Mothers in the community lived and met. While religious orders are governed externally by Church Fathers, they were also governed internally by a comparable structure of Church Mothers, the sisterhood's own divinely appointed superiors. There was one Mother Superior, or Superior General, several regional superiors also called Mother, and then every local convent had its own superior, some of whom were called Mother, too. Once you received the title of Mother in the convent, it stayed with you forever, even in death and on your tombstone.

Sisters' lives became governed by submissiveness to layers of "divine" authority, male and female alike. In the eyes of Church Fathers, nuns are to submit and obey without question all divinely appointed authority but their own. Even as recently as 1989, the papal commission reexamining the status of American Women Religious stressed obedience as the chief vow for nuns to follow and even flirted with the idea of having nuns return to religious habits.[2] When the Church Fathers forced sisters to change in the 1960s, the way we are today is not what they envisioned. The obedience of the sisterhood remains a source of tremendous concern to the Church Fathers, because when those silent, sleeping women wake, mountains will move. Within the submissive silence that nuns (and most Catholic women) have kept for years lay the power to change the world. And there's nothing more that the Church Fathers fear and abhor than the irreversible power of change, especially when it comes from women.

From the mid-nineteenth century when American sisterhood was born, until the mid-1960s when the whole world changed (in and out of the convent), the daily life of nuns pretty much remained the same. By papal decree all religious sisters were required to live in common; wear a habit; and profess vows of poverty, celibacy, and obedience. Some cloistered, contemplative nuns also vowed stability, vowed to remain in the convent house they entered, until death or departure. While some questionable religious practices were modified with time, common sense, and health codes (like kissing the floor, wearing wedding gowns for final profession, shaving heads), the sisterhood I entered in 1964 was not much different from the sisterhood of those women who entered fifty years before me. The biggest difference between the young and senior sisters lies in the fact that by 1964, much of what we were told to do made no sense. There were rules (like no talking) that we didn't take seriously or obey, nor were the consequences for breaking daytime silence serious. What may have worked in the sisterhood for a hundred years outlived its purpose. A big part of that was eighteen-year-old ignorance, and a big part of that was true.

Up until the Vatican Council II opened in 1963 (Pope John XXIII's divine mandate to change), convent life everywhere was uniformly and rigidly structured, censored, and supervised. All girls became initiated into sisterhood through a formation process that usually took seven years, seven being the number symbolizing completeness, fulfillment, and virginity, and in the Goddess religion the number seven represents the Great Mother. In a way, "sister formation" was a process of initiation into Great Motherhood, Great Sisterhood. For us, the seven years included nine long months as a postulant, two cloistered years in the novitiate, and two years of further study called the scholasticate, in which we completed our college education. Following graduation, we were sent out on "mission" the next day, giving us at least two years of living and working as real sisters before deciding to profess final vows.

At each stage of initiation, we looked more like real nuns. For nine months we were dressed as a postulant, which looked like a pilgrim. As postulants we wore floor-length black dresses and capes with white collars and, whenever we were in the chapel or left the building, black veils with narrow white headbands. Upon entering the novitiate we received the holy habit and for the first time looked like a "real nun." As a Sister of the Holy Cross, we sewed by hand our own habits according to *Constitutions of the Congregation:*

> The religious habit of black material is made as directed. It consists of a fitted waist and a gathered skirt which falls to a length of two inches from the ground; sleeves twelve inches wide extending to the finger tips; a circular cape reaching two inches below the waist and made of the same material as the habit skirt; small close fitting sleeves; a white collar. The headdress of white material consists of a small inner cap, a band to cover the forehead, and a circular border. A semi-circular black veil completes the headdress.
>
> The professed sister also wears a blue cincture, and a silver heart-shaped medallion surmounted by a cross. The medallion bears on its obverse image the image of the Mother of Sorrows and the words, *Congregatio Sancte Crucis* and on its reverse the words *Mater Dolorosissima, ora pro nobis.*[3] It is worn suspended on a black cord. The chaplet of seven dolors is worn at the right side. The chaplet is strung on a brass chain and has a cross of wood edged with brass bearing the corpus of Christ in the same metal.
>
> The novice wears a white veil . . . and receives the cincture and the silver heart at her first profession.[4]

For hundreds of years, girls were initiated into every Catholic sisterhood in nearly the same way. And though sister formation was modified in my day to ensure that we were qualified at the start to teach or nurse (it took some sisters more than ten years to finish college), the life we lived as nuns in training was as old as the community itself.

The order of the day for sisters remained the same for ages and remained relatively uniform throughout the Catholic sisterhood. Probably every nun in the world was wakened at 5:00 A.M. by the morning bell and followed the same schedule of events. Every sister I meet lived the same religious life I did. The order of our day was filled with spiritual exercises. Morning prayer and meditation were followed by mass and praying the Divine Office (psalms the whole church prays at certain times of the day). Then there was an examination of our consciences at noon (*particular examen*), praying the rosary, visiting the Blessed Sacrament (chapel visits), spiritual reading (*lectio divina*), and night prayer. Until the 1960s, that's what a day in the life of a nun looked like, with housework and ministry added.

When the fifty of us postulants weren't in the chapel doing spiritual exercises, we were given assigned housework, cleaning jobs called "obediences" because you had to do them whether you liked it or not. Everything we were asked to do was to be heard as a call from God, an obedience. For example, I spent one very hot Indiana summer working alone outside pulling weeds out of the cracks in the sidewalk and scrubbing bird droppings off picnic tables (an example of what happened to sisters who couldn't keep the silence). Every day (except Sunday) included at least an hour or two of manual labor. That's why convents always looked sparkling clean. Floors were waxed monthly on hands and knees, and buffed to shine every day. Each summer endless flights of ten-foot-wide staircases were sanded and varnished by hand. Manual labor was seen as no less holy a work than anything else we did. Even so, my not-so-holy sentiments while sweating on the hot sidewalk were similar to those of

Teresa of Avila when she got thrown from her horse into a big puddle of mud. To God she says: "If this is how you treat your friends, it's no wonder you have so few."[5]

The time that was left after spiritual exercises and housework was given to private prayer, study, creative work (music, art, writing, etc.), and recreation. Putting it all together, a day in the life of a sister looked like this:

5:00	A.M.	Rising Bell
5:30	A.M.	Morning Meditation
6:00	A.M.	Mass and Morning Prayer (Lauds)
7:00	A.M.	Breakfast (in silence)
8:00	A.M.	Housework
9:00	A.M.	Class/Study
11:45	A.M.	Examination of Conscience
12:00	P.M.	Lunch (in silence)
12:45	P.M.	Recreation
1:30	P.M.	Class/Study/Private Prayer
5:30	P.M.	Evening Prayer (Vespers)
6:00	P.M.	Dinner (usually in silence)
6:45	P.M.	Recreation
7:30	P.M.	Night Prayer (Compline)/Grand Silence
9:00	P.M.	Lights Out

Throughout that day, sisters' lives were wrapped completely in silence, enclosure, and censorship. We could not have been more separated from the rest of the world, nor could we have been more silent. With the exception of times appointed for "legitimate recreation," we were expected to keep quiet. As the rule book wisely noted, "Conversational powers are no common gift, especially among women meeting daily in the same circle." I suppose the founding sisters thought that since we did everything together, day after day, what was there to say? Not to mention the practical fact of how noisy the convent would be if fifty college-age women talked all the time, or laughed out loud as much as we did internally.

Silence was both a divine right and a divine rule in every sisterhood I know. We ate our meals in silence (except for special occasions) and worked in silence. And unless absolutely necessary, breaking silence was equivalent to a sisterly sin, something to be confessed at the monthly Chapter of Faults—a community exercise in sisterly humility. Of utmost importance was the silence to be kept at night, fittingly called the Great Silence, or Grand Silence. Beginning with the close of evening recreation and lasting until after mass the following morning, Great Silence was to be especially observed, so much so that breaking it was grounds for immediate dismissal. Even eye contact and sign language counted as a violation of Grand Silence. The belief was that sisters living in the presence of God would never disturb one another unnecessarily, especially at night, when Gods tend to speak more clearly. I still find myself keeping Grand Silence at night, though mine begins much later now, as does my rising.

Not only were our religious lives lived in silence, but they were also enclosed and isolated from outside influences, including family, friends, and all forms of media. Newspapers and magazines were banned, as was television and radio. While there was a large TV set in the community room (living room), the knobs were removed lest we be tempted to sneak a peek. I would have. Seeing any television program was a rare treat, and for the Sisters of the Holy Cross, Notre Dame football games were defined as one of them. One superior "Superior," Holy Cross Sister Gertrude Sullivan, allowed us to watch *Mission Impossible* and the Academy Awards the year Barbra Streisand won the Oscar for *Funny Girl.* Other than that, our lives as sisters-in-formation were cut off completely from the outside world—so much so that in 1967, we were informed about the Vietnam War one morning after breakfast, along with the other announcements for the day.

All the news we received as sisters-in-formation was censored by the superior, including incoming and outgoing mail. Two letters, one of which must be sent to family, could be written per month on a single sheet of paper. All mail was sent unsealed through the superior. Oftentimes our outgoing letters were returned in order to be rewritten to reflect more clearly how happy we were. No complaining about the rules, the food, or sisters we didn't like. Incoming mail was censored as well, and some letters, especially from former boyfriends, were never received. No love letters allowed. Long letters from best friends and family were equally troublesome. Most often, we'd receive only the first and last pages, the rationale being that anything really important would be said in those two parts. The truth of the matter was that the superior didn't have time to read it all, so we just got the first and last pages. That's how seriously censored contact was with the outside world. All correspondence was supervised and any attempt at "clandestine activity" (sneaking letters in and out) was grounds for immediate dismissal.

Until one was finally professed, immediate dismissal was always a daily threat, and any hint of scandal, especially anything sexual, provided clear and sufficient reason. Zero tolerance for sexual relationships in the sisterhood was a foregone conclusion long before I arrived on the scene, and every sister I talk to says the same. Even though incidents of sexual activity may occur, the minute it becomes public knowledge in the community, the sisters are gone. Because of the silence some nuns keep, stories can always be heard of sexual activity that goes on undetected and generally unknown, or known by a highly secretive few and generally ignored by the rest.

In asking sisters and former sisters if they were aware of sexual relationships in the sisterhood, I received two responses: yes and no. Some ex-nuns told stories about their sexual relationships of which no one was aware, including me. One sister spoke of being shocked and horrified by the seductive moves of her piano teacher (still a nun), and nearly all described the incidents as being so discreet and wrapped in silence that no one knew but the sisters involved. Most reported that they knew of no incidents of sexual activity, other than that of sisters who got sent home. All emphasized the zero-tolerance policy for sexual relationships in the sisterhood. Unacceptable.

Even with the universal zero-tolerance policy for sexual relationships in the Catholic sisterhood, the stories told in the 1985 revolutionary (at the time) book *Lesbian Nuns: Breaking Silence,* appear to be typical of the kind of sexual activity that occurred.[6] Fifty-two true stories are told of ex-nuns my age and their sexual escapades in the convent, some of which involved superiors and novice mistresses who remained community leaders. One former sister tells the story of being seduced by a "dear friend" of Mother Superior who dropped by her room one evening. "Finding Mother Superior out, she stayed to talk to me. In the wee hours of the morning, I realized that a woman was FLIRTING with me."[7] Having been invited to spend the night at "her place," and two whiskey sours later, she had her first sexual experience. Both women left the community shortly after, as did the Mother Superior and several other nuns in that convent who carried on sexual liaisons, one with a Franciscan monk.

Another ex-nun tells the story of having a sexual relationship with the postulant mistress who had been in the community for twenty years; both also left the convent eventually.[8] Several stories told of superiors who knew, but said and did nothing. Here is one such recollection:

> One morning the crude-mannered superior accosted me in the kitchen before Morning Prayer just as I finished putting the milk in the refrigerator.
>
> "Did you spend the night in Sister Martin's room last night?" she asked, shaking a finger at me. My heart stopped. What could I say? I knew that visiting another sister's room was forbidden.
>
> "Yes, Sister Superior," I answered, looking her in the eye and feigning a calmness I did not feel. . . . I waited for the anger and punishment I knew would come, but the Superior turned on her heel and left. She never mentioned it again.[9]

And nearly all talked about being "haunted" by the vow of chastity and eventually leaving the sisterhood. The young nun who spent the night with Sister Martin spoke of leaving the community because "the guilt lingered until I could no longer ignore the contradictions embodied in my relationship." She also reports, "more than once," that it was a priest who offered to "purge her" of her attraction to women.

Only one story told of a sister who remained in the convent while maintaining a sexual relationship by creating her own "alternative community." All of her relationships were highly secretive, and at that time she had been a sister for twenty-six years. Even she admitted, "I think I'm pushing the limits in terms of the community knowing about our relationship."[10] All admitted that even given their experiences of sexual relationships, they would never say that the convent is a hotbed of lesbianism. Repeatedly they admit that the structures just aren't there to support it. No one reported or knew of sexual relationships with anyone other than nuns and a handful of priests—no children, no teenagers, and no pursuing anonymous sex outside of the convent. For all of the sisters, their sexual partners were either priests or one another. We do not see in the sisterhood today the sexual permissiveness and scandal so prevalent in the priesthood because it's not there and hasn't been there for a very long time.

The only story I know of institutional abuse by nuns was revealed recently in Dublin, Ireland, with the Magdalene Asylums, the last of which was closed in 1996. According to a November 28, 2002, *New York Times* article, the Magdalene Asylums were set up in the nineteenth century by the Sisters of the Good Shepherd as a refuge for "fallen" women in Ireland, where according to Dublin reporter Sarah Lydall, "women who offended the country's moral code were sent to live, and sometimes die in disgrace."

> The nuns in charge proved to be a cruel lot. The girls were made to work seven days a week, 364 days a year (they get Christmas off), given little food, discouraged from forming friendships, beaten for minor infractions, humiliated and ridiculed, and worst of all forbidden to leave the home or make contact, even by letter, with the outside world.[11]

The Magdalene Sisters (which won the Best Film award at the 2002 Venice Film Festival) chronicles how abusive the nuns were to women in these asylums, which proved to be nothing more than slave-labor camps. The Vatican, true to form, denounced the film as "an angry and rancorous provocation," but as Lydall observes, "with so many scandals and investigations percolating at once here, it's not surprising that the film has stirred not a peep from the Catholic leadership in Ireland." So much for the Vatican's continuous claims that sexual abuse in the Catholic Church is an American phenomenon. While sexual abuse and humiliation were undoubtedly present in the Magdalene Asylums, it's the physical cruelty and psychological torture of women that appear to be the "abuse of choice" by nuns. As one theologian commented, "I really do think that sexual abuse is far more a man's problem. Nuns may be guilty of being better at psychologically and emotionally abusing others, but as for sex, I do think that's the man's method." Having been knuckle-whacked myself, I agree wholeheartedly.

For as mysterious and set apart as sisters were, not one of us could have anticipated what would happen all of a sudden in the mid-1960s, when the Church Fathers through Vatican II ask the Church Mothers (though not themselves) to change. All in the Catholic sisterhood were called to return to the holy spirit of their founders and change their religious and apostolic lives accordingly. As a result, the sisterhood has never been the same. While you can still find a handful of religious orders whose community lives resemble the schedule of the day we lived in 1964, and monastic orders remaining true to their cloistered calling, radical changes transformed every other sisterhood in this country by the late 1960s. Our dress code changed, our work changed, and our community lifestyle changed; everything about our lives as sisters changed quickly. Most important of all, our thinking and our understanding of religious life and community life changed. Within a few years, the sisterhood as we've always known it turned into the sisterhood we know today.

Almost immediately, we traded in our "Sister Mary . . ." names and took our family names back. I traded in Sr. Mary Carol Joseph and happily retrieved Karol Ann Jackowski. It felt like I got back my self. Everyone I knew (except for some senior sisters), gladly welcomed trading in the holy habit for something wholly more comfortable and far less conspicuous. In 1964, I was silent (sort of), censored, and enclosed, dressed from head to toe in several layers of black and white. In 1969, I graduated from college in a stylish navy blue knit suit, with plain shoulder-length blue veil. The night before, I even partied with my classmates, all of whom I was forbidden to talk to until that year. That's how quickly hundreds of years of tradition changed in the sisterhood. Literally overnight. And that's how suddenly heartbreaking those changes were to all the sisters for whom that was the only religious life they knew and loved. Many sisters wept silently for years over being forced to change in ways they didn't want to. I suspect some still do.

Within a few years our lives moved quickly from those of silent, cloistered, enclosed young sisters to those of socially active college students. And in convents all over the country something similar was happening. Once cut off from the world, sisters were now part of the world, and clearly glad to be back. In convents throughout the country, community life, which was once so uniform and regulated, became reorganized to better serve the needs of local sisters. Being able to wake up later was a dream-come-true. Called by the Holy Spirit of our founders to be silent and submissive no more, sisters began thinking for themselves in ways that were once outlawed. After not having to make decisions for years, all of a sudden we were asked to take part in every decision that affected our lives. Even Mother Superiors gave up their titles, and soon each convent was electing its own superior, now called coordinator, and a council (several nuns to manage household business). What transformed the sisterhood more than anything else in the 1960s was how quickly and obediently sisters responded to the divine experience of speaking their minds and governing themselves. It appeared as though some sacred fire, extinguished for years, had been reignited. The transformation that happened to the Church Mothers in the 1960s is unlike anything the sisterhood has ever seen, the effects of which we are still trying to discern.

Since the late 1960s, more than 300,000 nuns have left the sisterhood (one in five worldwide), "a breathtaking statistic," according to Elizabeth Abbott, one that "people in the Catholic circle call the 'bleeding'"[12] — the slow but steady loss of lifeblood from the Catholic Church. During that time, vocations in Europe and the United States also dropped by 50 percent. Of my class of fifty who entered the convent in 1964, three of us remain in the sisterhood. Today there are approximately eighty thousand nuns in the United States. The median age is near seventy and rising quickly, with no new recruits in sight. Only in the Third World are vocations to the sisterhood rising, only in those countries where the status of women is very low. But in this country, when we look at sisterhood now, we are looking at another precious endangered species.

What happened? Why did everyone leave? Why won't anyone join? The more ordinary our religious lives became as nuns, the more the mystique was gone and all the identity that went with it. As sisters became more immersed in work other than church work, and appeared to live just as every other committed Christian woman did, the unique meaning of our lives as nuns became more obscure. Through the steady stripping away of those external features that defined and set us apart for centuries, these questions emerge: If we now live and work and look like everyone else, then why be nuns? Why the sisterhood? What's the difference?

For more than 300,000 of us there wasn't any difference. Most sisters I know left to marry, to pursue a lesbian lifestyle, or to live a more independent life. Either celibacy or obedience was the reason. For some sisters, religious life didn't change fast enough, and for others it would never change enough while still governed by Church Fathers and Canon Law. Of the sisters who left, many are still living the religious life they wanted, either alone or in partnership with others. There are thousands of free-spirited ex-nuns still living religious lives in sisterhood with others, some celibately so. While the mystery that holds us together as nuns in this world appears to be vanishing, I see something else going on. At a time when sisterhood in the Catholic Church seems to be bleeding to death, I see signs of what looks like new life.

Hardly anyone is joining the Catholic sisterhood today because no fresh insight has emerged yet for doing so, and the demographics point to its impending demise. I met a bright, young, energetic woman who was affiliated with a religious order for three years, even lived with them for a year. On the day of her reception into the community, at mass on the altar, she realized what she was doing and announced to the congregation that she couldn't. A powerful movement of the Holy Spirit, I'd say. For as much as she loved and revered the sisters who were so overjoyed to accept her, so, too, could she see a sisterhood without peers, without companionship, without a future. She stood on the altar before her sisters and proclaimed to them what all sisterhood-seeking women must feel when they look at life as a nun now: "I'm sorry, but I just can't join your sisterhood." A powerful voice of the Holy Spirit, I'd say.

Because so many in sisterhood today are aging and uncertain of its future, women I meet are not inclined to think of religious life as sisterhood. Nor are they attracted to sisterhoods whose religious authority is subordinate to and dependent upon that of the Church Fathers. *Self-governing* and *independent* are the essential ingredients women tend to look for in sisterhood. At least that seems to be the case among the women I meet. Silent and submissive no more, most women I know are searching for an entirely different kind of religious sisterhood, one in which independence is preserved as the sacred inner fire that it is.

While sisterhood today does indeed appear to be bleeding to death with no future beyond its current aging members, the work that remains to complete its transformation is no less important, timely, or divinely inspired than what we did in our habited heyday. Even more important now, I believe, is the work of sisters, in providing the divine link to a new vision of sisterhood that will surely follow. As the silent, submissive voice of sisters strengthens and speaks, and as more continue to exercise their priestly powers, new forms of sisterhood are bound to rise from all that sacred spilled blood. And new forms of sisterhood are bound to attract thousands of women seeking that kind of soulful liberation, just as women did in the Jesus Movement. While we are clearly witnessing today the end of sisterhood as we've known it, we are also witnessing every day its rebirth, a sisterhood the likes of which we've never seen.

One divine sign of sisterhood to come appeared in the spring of 1970, at the height of the Nun Exodus from religious life. While hundreds of thousands of women left the convent because they didn't want to be nuns anymore, not all felt that way. Many sisters who left their orders (or were asked to leave) really didn't want to leave religious life at all; they just wanted to live it differently. Many treasured still the vows that bound them as sisters, but envisioned new ways of living poverty, celibacy, and obedience. Hundreds of sisters who felt that way, from many different communities, came together in the spring of 1970 under the inspired leadership of Sr. Audrey Kopp, well-known sociologist and anthropologist, and called themselves Sisters for Christian Community. Out of the 300,000 who left the convent, a handful continued to live as sisters anyhow, only differently. Out of all the bleeding from the nuns who left, a new kind of sisterhood was already born, almost immediately.

Very much in the Holy Spirit of the Beguine sisterhood, these new sisters, by divine communal intent, became a noncanonical Christian community, meaning that they are self-governing and not subject to the Canon Laws that rule all religious order (thus not "real nuns"). In 1970, these Sisters for Christian Community (SFCCs) envisioned a self-governing sisterhood as necessary for the survival of religious life into the twenty-first century and defined their community life accordingly. The founding of this new community was built solely on the holy beliefs of its sisters in full equality and self-governance. If sisterhood is to survive, independence and self-governance appear as its most amazing and saving grace, its heart and soul.

Just like the Beguines, the SFCCs have no motherhouse, no superiors, no subordinates, and hold nothing in common other than their beliefs. All are self-supporting, tax paying, and self-governing. Living alone or with others, communities form intentionally, gather regularly, and keep in touch just as loving families do—through personal contact, monthly meetings, bimonthly community newsletters, and annual international assemblies. Like the Beguinages throughout Europe, small SFCC communities can be found in Canada, Mexico, Central and Latin America, Western Europe, the British Isles, Africa, Guam, the Philippines, Australia, and the United States. Just as in the good old days, these new sisters are also like God; they, too, are everywhere, but they don't look different. They don't look anything like nuns at all.

The sisterhood we see today is unlike any we've seen before. Even the Beguines wore habits. The manner of SFCC sisterhood is so ordinary that we can't see the difference between them and us, at least not until we get up close and personal. That's when we can tell that these women are sisters by the way they love and care for one another, and the way they love and care for everyone who crosses their path. That's the only difference that matters. It's the single-hearted way that sisters love and work that sets them apart, and therein lies all the difference in the world.

Pure and simple, loving one another and building Christian communities is the mission of the SFCCs. In whatever work a sister does, be it religion or retail, her real job is to promote and witness Christian community, to encourage ways that are loving and just. As sisters we spent every day building community with the best and worst of women. As community builders, you'd think we'd be experts. Sisterhood is the greatest grace we receive as nuns, and community building its greatest gift, the divine link to sisterhood in the twenty-first century. Community building is the work of a church in crisis. The work is the sisterly art of bringing people together, lifting spirits higher, treasuring differences as holy, and accepting as divine everything that happens. The Gospel is the rule of life in the SFCCs, and building Christian community our apostolic mission, just as it was in the early church, in the beginning of sisterhood.

I do believe, along with every poet who ever wrote it, that "in the end is our beginning." What looks like the end of sisterhood, is without a doubt the end of something we knew as "nun," a dying image we'll likely always treasure for all that it was (and wasn't). And when we look at sisterhood today, it's easy to see only the endangered species destined for extinction. All we can see is the end to what we've always known. But powerful forces of transformation are at work in everything that ends. Something else is beginning that we can't see yet because its manner is too ordinary, its vision not yet clear, and its meaning not at all literal. While the sisterhood has just begun to speak, something else is also happening. There is a sisterhood emerging in the church (and in the world) unlike anything we've seen. All kinds of sleeping women are waking, and all kinds of silences are being spoken. All kinds of sisterhood are being born, and this is just the beginning. Women worldwide have either had enough, or are beginning to. When it comes to the sisterhood of all women, we've only begun. What feels like the strong winds of a Second Pentecost are just beginning to move us in ways we've never known before.

PART THREE

The Second Pentecost

Introduction

BEFORE WE LOOK AT THE Second Pentecost, it's important to understand what happened in the first one. Pentecost is the Christian feast of the Holy Spirit's descent upon the apostles, celebrated fifty days after the resurrection of Jesus, ten days after Jesus' ascension into heaven. What happens in Pentecost is the fulfillment of Easter, the coming true of Jesus' promise never to leave us alone after his death, but to remain with us always. Pentecost becomes the birthday of the Christian Church, because that's the day on which Jesus' Holy Spirit was "poured out on all humankind" (Acts 2:17). And what we celebrate on the Feast of Pentecost is the gift of the Holy Spirit intended for absolutely everyone. It's a powerful experience of God for those who receive it, so much so that the lives of those who do become transformed in ways they cannot comprehend. That's how profoundly transforming the Holy Spirit can be—all of a sudden we become capable of doing things we've never done before.

> When the days of Pentecost came it found them gathered in one place. Suddenly from up in the sky came a noise like a strong, driving wind which was heard all through the house where they were seated. Tongues as of fire appeared, which parted and came to rest on each of them. All were filled with the Holy Spirit. They began to express themselves in foreign languages and

made bold proclamations as the spirit prompted them. (Acts 2:1–4)

A double miracle happens at Pentecost, two astounding experiences in one. Not only do the apostles begin to speak in foreign languages, but everyone listening to them "from every nation under heaven" understood what they were saying. Scripture tells us that everyone who gathered around the apostles became "very much confused because each one heard them speaking their own language" (Acts 2:6). Even Arabs understood what the apostles were saying about the "marvels God has accomplished" (Acts 2:11) and all were moved deeply by what they had heard. The apostles suddenly understood how to move the hearts and souls of those "from every nation under heaven" (Acts 2:5) and miracle of miracles, they were understood by everyone as well. In the first Pentecost, we see how understanding and being understood is a divine sign, a holy spirit, a loving signal that God is with us.

Scripture reveals that everyone gathered was "dumbfounded and could make nothing at all of what had happened" (Acts 2:12). Many even thought the apostles were drunk or on drugs. The experience of God can have that effect. It can literally transform lives in ways no one can explain, least of all those touched powerfully by the Holy Spirit. The miracle of the whole world hearing and understanding these "tongues" is a divine sign of the universal call of the church, the inclusive gift of Christianity poured out on all humankind. Even Arabs, pagans, and Cretans understood the message. That's how powerful the Holy Spirit can be when spoken in truth. We begin to understand one another and begin to be understood, the main ingredient of world peace (and a world religion). Understanding and being understood emerges as a primary priestly power in the first Pentecost.

What happens in Pentecost is a sign of things to come whenever followers of Christ become moved by the Holy Spirit. Diverse religions from all over the world come together and find themselves united, find themselves understanding one another like never before. Seen as the "Pentecost of the pagans," some three thousand joined the Jesus Movement that day, all of whom "devoted themselves to the apostle's instruction and the communal life, to the breaking of the bread and the prayers" (Acts 2:42). In the first Pentecost all are united as one in the Holy Spirit of Christ. No one is excluded. The impossible dream of worldwide unity became reality. The double miracle of speaking and understanding one another's language emphasizes the fact that the first Christian community was extended to include all people, a Holy Spirit given to be borne to the ends of the earth. The Holy Spirit of excluding no one becomes another priestly power given in Pentecost. In excluding no one, Jesus becomes one with everyone, and in that way becomes divine. His Holy Spirit is poured out on all humankind in Pentecost so that "All may be one" (John 17:20).

In giving birth to the Christian church, Pentecost is an intense religious experience loaded with meaning about what kind of "church" Jesus had in mind. In the first Pentecost, we see the gift of new life given to the Christian community, a new law of God, a whole new creation. Pentecost is all about getting new hearts and having a new spirit rise within us, bringing us new ways of thinking, feeling, living, and loving. It's about the inner power of the Holy Spirit and all the re-creation (and recreation) that happens naturally in our lives as a result. In the fullness of time, which is now just as much as it was then, the Holy Spirit descends into everyone, "poured out on *all* humankind." In that miraculous outpouring of love, Jesus completes his work on earth. The rest is up to us. The mission to renew the life of the church is ours, all of ours. And never, it seems, have we been more in need of a power like that of a Second Pentecost than right now. Both in the Catholic Church and in the world, all we seem to know is the power of divisiveness and violence in the name of God. We are void of the Holy Spirit to understand and be understood. And we are void of the Holy Spirit that excludes no one. All that seems to move us is the power of a spirit that appears to be everything else but holy.

Perhaps now more than ever, Pentecost presents itself to us as a divine mystery we are desperately in need of entering once again. An outpouring of the Holy Spirit on all humankind is the only movement capable of transforming the hearts of stone that have defiled and betrayed the Catholic Church. An outpouring of the Holy Spirit is the only movement that can fulfill Ezekiel's "dry bones" prophecy of bringing the dispersed, scattered, broken, and nearly dead church back together again, back to divine life.

> Dry bones, hear the word of the Lord! Thus says the Lord God to these bones: "See! I will bring spirit into you, that you may come to life. I will put muscle upon you, make flesh grow over you, cover you with skin nd put spirit in you that you may come to life." Even as I was prophesying . . . I heard a noise, it was a rattling as the bones came together, bone joining bone . . . I saw the muscle and flesh come upon them and the skin cover them. . . . Then from the four winds a spirit came into them; they came alive and stood upright, a vast army. (Ezek. 37:1–10)

Having had the name of God profaned by the highest priests of the Catholic Church, nothing but a Holy Spirit can bring us back to divine life again, no matter how much the Church

Fathers try to force us back to the way we were, blindly obedient and saintly submissive. What happened at the first Pentecost, we need desperately to happen again. The Catholic Church and all humankind have never been in need of spiritual union as we are now, and never has a Second Pentecost become a more heartfelt prayer. "Veni Sancte Spiritu" is the church's prayer on the Feast of Pentecost, just as it's become a daily prayer now. Come, Holy Spirit, come.

In order to understand exactly what we're asking for when we pray for the Holy Spirit to come again, it's important to realize what *spirit* is and what a Holy Spirit can do to our hearts and souls. In the second story of creation, the Book of Genesis reveals that God blew into our nostrils the breath of life, and so we became living beings (Gen. 2:7). In blowing the breath of life into us, we are given the Holy Spirit of God. We become full of holy spirits. That's what brings us to life, and that's how dramatically our lives change when we are guided by our holy spirits. As long as the breath of life is in our body, we are all, as the nuns taught us, Temples of the Holy Ghost, Temples of Sacred Fire. Male and female, believer and unbeliever, Muslim, Jew, and Christian, we all bear the Spirit of God within us. We are all born of One Holy Spirit. We are all born with the divine power to love. All faces are the faces of God.

In revealing God's image and likeness as the breath of life, we see that the Holy Spirit is just as essential to our daily life as is breathing. Without it we feel dead, lifeless, and meaningless. When we refuse to recognize the Holy Spirit in ourselves and in one another, when we refuse to see in one another the face of God, that's when our lives begin to go wrong. That's when we become abusive, mean-spirited, corrupt, and destructive of all that is holy. That's when our hearts turn to stone and we turn to everything that serves to harden the hearts of others. We become incapable of understanding those who are not like us, and incapable of experiencing any of life as divine, especially love, the Holiest Spirit of all. That's how essential Pentecost and the Holy Spirit are in our life, the life of the church, and in all humankind. There can be no such thing as Holy Communion without it. There can be no such thing as church.

How the Spirit of God comes to us today is just as divine a mystery as it was then. Throughout Scripture, one of the ways God communicates with us is in the form of fire, a fire often associated with breath or wind. It's no wonder then that the author of the Acts of the Apostles would use the images of wind and fire to explain what happened to them. In Pentecost, the Holy Spirit appears first as a "strong driving wind," followed by "tongues of fire." Divine mystery surrounds the apostles in the form of wind, and divine revelation follows in the form of fire, "tongues of fire" that come to rest upon them. The Holy Spirit appears as that over which the apostles have no control, and that which suddenly transforms their lives. They were just as dumbfounded over the instant ability to speak different languages as were those who understood them clearly. Arabs and Christians understood one another perfectly. That's how surprising and personally transforming the Holy Spirit can be in those upon whom its divine power rests. Not even they knew what came over them. It was a miracle.

Far more than a miraculous Bible story, the account of Pentecost is an attempt to explain all the unexplainable events that can happen when our lives are moved by holy spirits. Transformed from the inside out, we, too, become capable of extraordinary and miraculous works. Even without expecting anything special, and even without any preparation, the apostles' lives and personalities become suddenly and totally changed. With all the unpredictable suddenness of wind and fire they are rendered capable of communicating in a new and more powerful way.

In the first Pentecost we see that simply being chosen as apostles is not enough. No amount of ritual anointing or ordaining can make us priestly people. Nor can the sacrament of Holy Orders make a bad man a good priest. While the church teaches that immoral and criminal priests can still deliver good sacraments, the Holy Spirit (and all humankind) begs to differ. A more penetrating action of the Holy Spirit becomes absolutely necessary, without which we can do nothing in the name of God and everything contrary and destructive to the works of the Holy Spirit: peace, patience, joy, love, kindness, generosity, faithfulness, gentleness, and self-control (Gal. 5:22–23a)—all of which have become an endangered species. Without the loving power of those holy spirits, we are literally good for nothing but no good at all. If we were ever in need of a Second Pentecost to be poured out on all humankind, I'd say that time is right now. ASAP.

The Holy Spirit who transformed completely the lives of the apostles (and the three thousand who joined them that day) is none other than that of the power of love, the Holy Spirit of Jesus Christ remaining with them. Accompanying them wherever they go and guiding everything they do, the Holy Spirit becomes a powerful source of inspiration and strength for the apostles. Everything in their life changes, especially the way they see and the way they understand. Their literal-thinking ways become transformed by the Pentecost Spirit and the whole world looks different. The apostles became ministers of a new covenant, a new kind of law, and a new kind of religious experience. The old way of understanding God's laws literally gives way to a new kind of understanding, one in which we are guided by the spirit of love.

It's the letter of the law and understanding God's word literally that kills the love and understanding in which divine laws are given, and kills the Holy Spirit in the souls of those who receive and understand the laws of God literally. Such fundamentalism, so rampant in organized religions (Catholicism included), mostly serves to sanctify ignorance, mandate mediocrity, and justify every personal reason we have to judge and exclude, even hate and kill one another in the name of our God. Scripture reveals that the letter of the law and its literal interpretation are not what Jesus Christ had in mind. Only the spirit of love gives life to the laws of God, the Holy Spirit in which they were given. Anything but love serves to kill the real intent of God. So dead and void of love are many of the church's teachings (especially with regard to women and sex) that few continue to follow them, the priesthood included.

The Holy Spirit who gives new life to the laws of the church and its makers is none other than what the Gospel of Saint John calls the Paraclete, the Holy Spirit of truth. All biblical revelations of truth are founded on the experience of a profound encounter with God (like that of a Pentecost), which is to say that the Holy Spirit within gives each of us knowledge of God and insight into the hidden truth (or will of God) behind everything that happens. It's the Holy Spirit who enables us to see what's really going on and enables us to say truthfully what we see. Like the apostles at the first Pentecost, those possessed by the Spirit are led to 'make bold proclamations as the spirit prompts them . . . about the marvels God has accomplished." Only those led by holy spirits receive divine revelations and have access to divine truths. The literal-minded remain soulfully blind. They are the blind who lead the blind because only the blind follow them.

Almost always, the silence we keep is nothing other than the Holy Spirit of truth, some truth we will not tell, for some reason cannot tell, or feel bound completely from telling. In banning and punishing dissent from church teaching as divisive and evil (heresy), the Church Fathers also, in effect, condemn as divisive and evil the Holy Spirit of truth. Because we can only be made holy in the truth (John 17:1), it's only the truth that can set us free from the silence that threatens to kill the Holy Spirit in the people once and for all. And it's only the truth now that can restore the Catholic Church to the holiness it knew in the beginning, the good old holy days when those who led the Christian Church were themselves led by the Holy Spirit, led only by their love of God and one another, and empowered by the miraculous ability to understand and be understood. The silence we keep about the truth behind the corruption we see in the Catholic Church is part and parcel of the letter of the law that kills the spirit of truth. Behind every kept silence lies a divine truth bound to be set free by the Holy Spirit. And by the power of a Second Pentecost, we are bound to transform and restore to full Holy Communion this church torn apart and scattered by the crimes and sins of its fathers. By the power of the Holy Spirit, that's bound to happen.

What is truth? We know truth when we hear it because it strikes a heartfelt chord in our souls. It makes divine sense to us. It moves us in such a profound way that we are led to follow wherever the truth takes us, even through fear, misery, and suffering. Truth is a language understood by those possessed by the Holy Spirit, regardless of race, gender, or religion. The Gospel of Saint John reveals, "You know Christ and recognize him because he dwells within you" (John 14:17). Accordingly, it's the Holy Spirit within us all who moves our hearts and souls to recognize the truth when we hear it and see it. And it's the spirit of evil within us who refuses to see the truth and does all in its power to bind everyone in silence in order to protect and keep hidden its evil ways. As free spirits, we are fully capable of being both good and evil. We are capable of being guided by holy spirits, as well as choosing to silence them by doing all in our power to suppress truth and paralyze its works. In that way we become devil's advocates, so to speak, those who feed the faithful with lies instead of truth in the name of God, those who appear no longer capable, as one Catholic described, of even recognizing the truth, "even if it came up and bit them in their clerical arse."

It makes sense that those who believe in God become inhabited by the Holy Spirit of the God in whom they believe. As Christians, the world knows us by the way we love one another, by our inclusiveness, and by our ability to understand and be understood. So, too, with those who believe in the power of privilege, secrecy, silence, lies, and the infallible letter of their laws, they are inhabited by the unholy spirits in which they believe. We know a tree by its fruit, and given the fruit of the Catholic priesthood we see, only a Second Pentecost can save us. At least that's how it appears to me. Only an inner transformation as profound as that of the first Pentecost is capable of bringing to new life all the dry dead bones and clerical hearts of stone. And only an outpouring of a Holy Spirit on all humankind can ever save the whole world from the total destruction we are so hell-bent on pursuing in the name of our Gods. A Second Pentecost is what the whole world needs now, and signs of its second coming are beginning to appear, at least among the dissenting faithful People of God, evermore the heart and soul of the Catholic Church.

While the Holy Spirit may appear silent and inactive, the truth of the matter is that far more is going on than meets the eye. Behind the scenes, we see the Holy Spirit moving the faithful to connect with one another, support one another, and speak the truth to one another. Extraordinary and unprecedented movements among Catholics demanding the whole truth and nothing but the truth are clear signs of a Second Pentecost. Holy silent and blindly obedient no more, so many are being moved, even compelled, to speak the truth. A new Pentecost in the Catholic Church has begun. The community of the faithful is leading the way, with and without the support of the Church Fathers. We in the Catholic Church are experiencing all the divine signs of a Second Pentecost, and it's only a matter of time before the fullness of its transforming effects is realized.

A priesthood of the people is emerging with all the power of a Second Pentecost, just as the Christian community did in the beginning. And by the power of the same Second Pentecost, a sisterhood of all women is slowly waking and beginning to move the mountains of clerical deceit and betrayal heaped upon them by the Church Fathers. Silent and submissive no more, the Holy Spirit appears to be working overtime in us, urging truths to be spoken, and moving the Catholic Church to be transformed just as it was at the first Pentecost. A Second Pentecost is already driving its winds through the Catholic Church, and pouring itself out on all humankind. The rebirth of Catholicism has begun—a rebirth led now, as it was in the beginning, by the priesthood of the people and the sisterhood of all women.

7

The Priesthood of the People

IN EVERY RELIGION, PRIESTS are simply those responsible for their church, and in the Catholic Church, all those baptized share priestly responsibility. In baptism we are all called to priesthood; all of us are ordained to do something divine with our life, whether we choose to do so or not. While those who exercise priesthood in an ordained capacity have specific sacramental responsibilities, it's the whole community of believers who make up any church. Without the Christian community (in and out of the pew), ordained priesthood has little meaning and no priestly function. Vatican II could not have been any more clear in its divine message that the People of God are the church just as much as its priests are. Without a community of believers gathered around the table, there can be no communion, no church, and virtually no priesthood. The most essential element of any priesthood is the priesthood of the People of God.

In ancient religions, those called to priesthood by God and the people are given special responsibilities for the life of the church. Called to serve as leaders and ministers of the community at worship, they become keepers of the mysteries of God, guardians and trustees of the church's sacred rituals, traditions, and teachings. And they are recognized and received by the community as spokespersons of God, mediators between God and the people, those chosen to help us discern the will of God. In every church, its truly ordained priests are those in constant contact with God. They are the ones we turn to when we are in need of divine intervention. The most sacred and important responsibility of any priest is that of remaining close to God. Like the vestal virgins, they are to keep a constant eye on the sacred fire burning within their own soul and that of the church. In failing to do so, like some vestal virgins, they are as good as being buried alive. They become far worse than good for nothing because *in persona Christi* they begin to use lies to proclaim the truth. In the Gospel of John, Jesus reveals that Satan is among us as the one who lies. "Lying speech is his native tongue," Jesus says. "He is a liar and the father of lies" (John 8:44). A frightening thought given what we know about the secrets and lies of the fathers.

Given the most sacred responsibilities in the church, the truly ordained priest emerges above all as one touched by God's Holy Spirit in an extraordinary way, one so close to God and so in touch with the people that he is ordained by both to exercise priestly leadership in the church. Those closest to God become chosen naturally to lead God's people because only they know how to do so. Only they understand and can be understood. Ordained or not, it's only closeness to God that can make a priest. There is no such thing as being a priest without it. In the mind of everyone but the Church Fathers, a bad man cannot be a good priest; one's character and morality have everything to do with the holiness of the sacraments we receive. That's why we hear such outrage from Catholics over pedophile priests remaining in the priesthood. Without an extraordinary closeness to God, those who assume the sacred responsibilities for the church are doomed to far more than personal failure. Not only do such priests deceive and betray the God in whose name they do everything, but so, too, do they deceive and betray the People of God as well, destroying the truth they are chosen to guard and protect as sacred.

When any priesthood fails in its divine responsibilities to God and the people, as so many Catholics now believe the Church

Fathers have, what happens in the community as a result is divine intervention with and without them. What we see happening today in the church is how clearly the Holy Spirit inhabits the soul of the people. Rising to meet the devastating consequences heaped upon Catholics by sins of its fathers, it's the priesthood of the people who are beginning to take upon themselves the responsibilities as community builders, ministers of prayer, guardians of sacred truths and traditions, and spokespersons of God. By the divine power of everything that looks like a Second Pentecost, the priesthood of the people is rising as ministers of a new kind of Catholic Church, a new kind of priesthood re-created in the image and likeness of Jesus Christ.

The priesthood of the people appears full of a Holy Spirit the likes of which we haven't seen since the first Pentecost. It's the priesthood of the people who appear most capable now of helping restore divine life to a church badly broken and betrayed by its Holy Fathers. By the power of what looks like a Second Pentecost, it's the people who've become the most understanding, the most inclusive, and the most understood. And it's the voice of the faithful that sounds most priestly, most like the voice of God.

✣ ✣ ✣

While Jesus never claims the title of priest for himself and invites everyone to participate in his ministry of service, so, too, does the priesthood of the people. Without ordination, and inclusive of everyone, a new priesthood is already being created by a divine intervention very much like that of a Second Pentecost. With all the divine power of a "strong, driving wind" sweeping across this country, the People of God are already building what looks like a new priesthood, a new church, a new understanding of church laws, and a new relationship between God, priesthood, and the people. Calling on one another to exercise our priesthood in rebuilding the Catholic Church is the first sign we see that the priesthood of the people, like that of Saint Paul in the early church, is moved in a divine way "to serve God in newness of Spirit" (Rom. 7:6). A Second Pentecost is already sweeping through the darkest corners of the Catholic Church, and nowhere is its Holy Spirit more alive than in the priesthood of its people.

What is the *priesthood of the people* and how is it different from that of the Church Fathers? From what I see, profound differences can be found in every important way. First and foremost, what I see among Catholics today is not a priesthood of privilege, and clearly not a people who believe that they are a divine law unto themselves. Perhaps the greatest scandal is how meticulously the Church Fathers have created a self-serving priesthood in which all Catholics (and the whole world) are expected to defer to their authority as divine, and comply with every request as though it comes directly from God. In a letter from a theologian who teaches seminarians, I was told:

> The biggest scandal, frankly, is the clerical culture of privilege. I see it even in our youngest seminarians. They have the attitude that because they are going to be priests, all things should be handed to them. Unfortunately, society often obliges!!! That is our "mea culpa"!!! It's that "privilege" that has allowed them to behave so badly and so secretively. They don't think there is any law bigger than themselves. Frankly, this is the most frightening evil of all.

Apparently that's the kind of priesthood the Catholic Church exercises, safeguards, and attracts. One in which the whole world is at their service with bowed heads, bended knees, and open pockets. One in which the whole world must believe that they are *in persona Christi,* acting as the person of Christ. They alone are like unto God, and the one and only true God at that. To this day the Church Fathers proclaim that there is no salvation outside the Catholic Church and its teachings, while the rest of the world now sees very little salvation in it. That's how disconnected the priesthood of privilege has become from that of the people. The Church Fathers have all but lost touch completely with the people they've been ordained to serve.

Unlike the priesthood of privilege, which is the only priesthood the Catholic Church has known, what I see emerging in the Christian community (good priests included) is a priesthood of service inspired by that of Jesus who reveals, "I am in the midst of you as one who serves" (Luke 22:27). Nowhere does Jesus establish a caste of rich, powerful, privileged men. Nothing could be further from divine truth. Serving and not being served is the essence of Jesus' "priesthood," and the Gospels are full of what it means to be a servant of God. Repeatedly we are shown how service of God excludes worship of anything else, "privilege" in particular, and everything that comes with it, especially money and the accumulation of wealth.

Jesus is clear in naming money and privilege as the biggest obstacles standing in the way of serving God. No one can serve those two masters at the same time. We cannot serve both God and a rich, privileged life in the mind of Jesus. Regardless of how hard we may try to use one to sanctify and justify the use of the other, Jesus reveals simply, "If you love one, you hate and despise the other" (Matt. 19:21). So much so that those who cling to and worship their privileged status have as much chance of getting close to God as a camel trying to stuff itself through the eye of a needle. In other words, fat chance. The priesthood of the people seeks service, not privilege.

The second striking difference between the priesthood of the people and the priesthood of privilege is that of inclusiveness. An essential part of every privileged group is the right it reserves as holy to exclude anyone and everyone unlike it. Privileged groups of men all over the world will go to their graves doing everything in their power to exclude women and minorities, excluding everyone not made in their image and likeness, anyone who may threaten all that they hold sacred and secret. While the ordination of women is inevitable in the Catholic Church, in the vehemently angry words of the Church Fathers, that will happen only over their dead bodies. Even so, it will happen, and given the average age of the Church Fathers, it's likely to happen a lot sooner than they believe. If death is what it takes for the Holy Spirit to be reborn again in the Catholic Church, then that will happen by the grace of God.

Exclusiveness has become a divine law in Catholicism's priesthood of privilege, an essential part of the sacrament of Holy Orders. It's not a matter at all, the Church Fathers proclaim, of not wanting to ordain women, it's just that God won't let them. It's God who, for some mysteriously divine reason, does not intend for women to exercise their priesthood in the Catholic Church. They say that excluding women is not their priestly idea, it's God's divine revelation. No women allowed. Ever. Like all exclusive societies who become laws unto themselves, so, too, do the Church Fathers become laws unto themselves in demanding an exclusively male priesthood; and so, too, do they identify their sexist beliefs as the infallible will of God.

Even so, few Catholics believe in a sexist God, and most Catholic theologians are revealing that the God of Jesus Christ had no such exclusively sexist intent at all. There is nothing divine in the revelation of the Church Fathers that women must be banned from priesthood. That is one church law of their own making and keeping, and clearly contrary to the Spirit of Christ revealed in Saint Paul's letter to the Galatians:

> All of you who have been baptized in Christ have clothed yourself with him. There does not exist among you Jew or Greek, slave or free, male or female. All are one in Christ Jesus. Furthermore, if you belong to Christ you are the descendants of Abraham, which means you inherit all that was promised. (Gal. 3:27–29)

The priesthood of the people I see emerging in the Catholic Church is just as adamant about its God-given inclusiveness as the Church Fathers are of their God-given exclusiveness. With all the mysterious power of a Second Pentecost, the priesthood of the people includes everyone called to the Christian life, and its decisions become ordained by acclamation, accepted as true by the voice of the faithful. Once priesthood stands in the midst of its community as one who serves, inclusiveness becomes its divine law and guiding principle. All are included because all bear within them a Holy Spirit and all speak to one another with the voice of God. In a priesthood of service it becomes the privilege of everyone to speak of the God they know, and the privilege of the Christian community to discern the voice of God they hold in common. As a result, no one becomes oppressed by the superior will or voice of another. All are liberated soulfully because that's what happens when all are treated as one. That's what happens when God is with us.

Because there is no secrecy in a priesthood of service, no one is bound by silence from speaking the truth. On the contrary, speaking the truth is what just gave birth to the priesthood of the people, and speaking the truth is the most divine law this new priesthood knows. With all the mysterious power of a Second Pentecost, the priesthood of the people appears guided by the Holy Spirit, demanding relentlessly of the Church Fathers nothing less that the whole truth. The victims of abuse who've been bound and battered by years of silence are embraced by the priesthood of the people, as is the painful truth they're beginning to reveal. The voice of everyone is treasured as sacred. No one is excluded, least of all women and children. All are welcome in the priesthood of the people because what binds them as one is not privilege and power, but heartfelt love and concern for one another. That's how we know any priesthood comes from God. Jesus reveals, "This is how all will know you for my disciples, by your love for one another" (John 13:35).

The third striking difference between the priesthood of the people and that of the Church Fathers lies in understanding how divine truth is revealed and what we do with what we hear as the "voice of God." In a priesthood built on privilege and power and strengthened by secrecy and silence, it's no wonder the Catholic Church grew into proclaiming itself and its teachings infallible. A big part of privileged priesthood is the unshakable belief in themselves as God on earth, Jesus Christ personified, and therefore the exclusive source of divine revelation. This kind of thinking is far more common among priests than we'd like to believe. I've listened to many priests preach at the Eucharist, and far too often the homily goes something like this. The Gospel of the day is read, and in his homily the priest tells a personal story, an experience he had, comparing what he did with what Jesus did in the Gospel. Fair enough. But it's always the conclusion the priest draws that's the most revealing. In comparing himself to Jesus, the priest sees only how much Jesus is like him. Jesus did what the priest did. And he speaks of it in the homily as a stunning insight. He is so like Jesus that Jesus is just like him. (Had he been just like Jesus he would not have been proclaiming his good works from the pulpit.) That's how the privileged priesthood hears the Word of God and their own—as one and the same, with God's voice sounding just like theirs. Given such a privileged vision of priesthood, how could they possibly be wrong? That's what the Church Fathers still can't understand.

Infallibility means the Catholic Church can do no wrong and is divinely incapable of error. Even Jesus is like them. When it comes to the divine revelation reflected in Catholic teaching, the Church Fathers can't possibly be wrong, regardless of the millions of Catholics (not to mention the rest of the world) who believe they are, and their own criminal thinking that proves repeatedly that they are. It's part of the privileged everywhere that their ways of thinking are designed to dominate, but in the Catholic Church the domination becomes packed with all the power of God. Not believing is never simply disagreement, or a matter of respectfully seeing the truth differently, it becomes sin, heresy, cause for excommunication, even death by Inquisition in the Middle Ages. Infallibility and unchanging truths are not the problem here; it's to whom they belong. That's the real problem. According to the Catholic doctrine of "receptivity," a teaching is true to the extent that the faithful accepts it as true; we all know a bit of the truth. In other words, infallibility belongs to the *whole* Catholic Church, not just its teaching fathers.

In the priesthood of the people, infallible truths are safeguarded as sacred, but where they come from and how they're revealed appears is entirely different from the priesthood of the elect. First of all, how we think about truth is far more dynamic and subject to further clarification from time to time. As we grow in knowledge, understanding, and consciousness, so, too, does our understanding of what's true change. A growing understanding of truth is completely unlike that of the Church Fathers whose thinking is fixed, static, and impossible to change, even infallible. The historian Garry Wills explains this new way of thinking as a process of moving from truth to truth. "The truth one leaves behind is not necessarily false, but a less adequate expression of truth that leads to a more adequate one."[1] Our knowledge of everything, including ourselves, grows and changes just as we grow and change in consciousness, in what we experience as true. In the priesthood of the people, change emerges as the most sacred and infallible truth they know. Change is a divine law of nature, a divine law of us, and a divine law of God.

How do we know what's true if the truth is always changing? In the words of Cardinal John Henry Newman (1859), the only true infallibility comes from "consulting the faithful in matters of doctrine."[2] It's the consensus of the people that reveals divine truth, the whole church revealing together where it is they see the Holy Spirit leading. Infallible truths (such as how sacred all life is) become clear when everyone begins to reveal what they see and hear when they listen in prayer and discern the movements of their Holy Spirit. While the Church Fathers continue to proclaim that Catholicism is no democracy, the Holy Spirit begs to differ. Why isn't it? We are all endowed with a soul that bears the divine life and voice of God. In the priesthood of the people infallible truths are found in hearing what the whole church experiences and knows as true. The voice of God is clearest when we listen to what everyone has to say, and not the voices of a self-ordained privileged few.

Change becomes a sacrament within the priesthood of the people because that's clearly how the Holy Spirit reveals divine truth. The truth doesn't change. It's we who change in our ability to understand truths more clearly. The more we refuse to change our thinking, the more resistant we become to the work of the Holy Spirit in ourselves and in one another. Our hearts become hardened and we refuse to listen to anyone (including the sacred voice of science) except our unchanging minds. Infallibility is no less precious or divine in the priesthood of the people, but where it comes from and to whom it belongs is profoundly different from that of the priesthood of privilege. With all the divine power of a Second Pentecost a new vision of divine truth is being revealed, one in which the sacred voice of everyone is heard, including that of "every nation under heaven." That's how inclusive the voice of divine truth is in the new priesthood. The more divine voices we hear from the people, the more clear and infallible are its sacred truths. In the coming of a Second Pentecost, the truths we treasure and keep sacred as infallible will be those that reflect the voice of God's people, and not the will of a privileged, exclusive, secretive few.

✝ ✝ ✝

The call to service, inclusiveness, and change is what appears to guide the priesthood of the people. Who are the people of this new priesthood? Where do they come from? They are everyone coming together because of the lies, the betrayal, and the devastation the church is suffering at the hands of its fathers. Bound by silence no more, the priesthood of the people are all those coming forward to say, "Enough!" By the power of the Holy Spirit, even judges, the courts, and the law of the land have had enough of these privileged fathers, their crimes, and their lies. Catholic and non-Catholic alike have become part of the priesthood of the people. All humankind is horrified over what's happening in the Catholic priesthood today.

Just as in the first Pentecost, so, too, are those of every belief coming together to cleanse the Catholic Church of its criminal thinking and bring her back to divine life. Even the law of the land appears to be driven by the same holy winds of change that are blowing through the deepest and darkest corners of the Catholic Church, forcing its priesthood to submit to laws higher than themselves. The priesthood of the people is strengthened by the divine laws of the land as well as the divine laws of God. Even those who aren't Catholic are driven and compelled to work to eliminate its criminal priestly abuses. That's how powerful the Second Pentecost already is, and it's just begun to pour out on all humankind.

Included in the priesthood of the people are the good priests who never staked their claim to privilege, exclusiveness, or infallibility, all the good priests who stand in the midst of the people as those who serve. No longer bound by silence, a handful of priests are joining their voices with those of the people. On November 17, 2002, the *Boston Herald* printed an article by Dominican priest and canon lawyer Fr. Thomas P. Doyle, in which he writes about the exceptions in the priesthood to all those involved in its lies, crimes, cover-ups, and silence:

> Notable among them is a parish priest from East Longmeadow, Mass., Father James Scahill, whose parish is withholding the 6% diocesan tax that goes to the bishop's office weekly and is used at his discretion. Scahill and his parishioners have made it clear that they will continue to withhold this tax until Father Richard Lavigne is laicized and no longer receives *any* compensation from the Diocese of Springfield.

> Father Lavigne pleaded guilty to child molestation in 1992. Later in 1992, the diocese settled a suit brought by 17 additional victims for $1.3 million. More than 10 years after his conviction, and in the face of additional lawsuits, Lavigne is still a priest, gets paid a salary by the diocese, and has fully paid medical insurance.
>
> As a canon lawyer I can state clearly that Bishop Thomas Dupre could have, and most importantly should have sought the forced laicization of Lavigne during the last 10 years; yet he has chosen to do nothing. . . . Bishop Dupre has been quoted as saying that the process is too "cumbersome"' and that even if he chooses to seek Lavigne's laicization, he will continue to pay him because canon law would force him to do so, and it is the charitable thing to do.
>
> There is nothing in canon law that forces him to do any such thing. . . . The reality is that almost without exception, laicized former priests, including John Geoghan, receive nothing from their dioceses precisely because of canon law. When are my fellow priests going to realize that there is something seriously wrong with this picture? When are they going to get out from behind the pulpit and let their communities know these actions and inactions are unconscionable?[3]

Among the priesthood of the people are the good church fathers like Tom Doyle who can no longer keep the silence that binds priests of privilege, regardless of the clerical price they are likely to pay. In 1986, Father Doyle, a prophet way ahead of his time, stood before his canon lawyer brethren and named priestly pedophilia as the greatest problem that we in the church have faced in centuries. Shortly after, he was removed from his position at the Vatican Embassy in Washington, D.C. (the road to becoming bishop), and lost his teaching position in canon law at Catholic University. That's the price priests can expect to pay for breaking the silence, and that's why so few are willing to do so. Father Doyle is currently serving as an air force chaplain in Germany and is still speaking out against the sinful silence of his brothers.

Sad but true, the loss of priestly privilege is too high for many, which reveals where the essence of their priesthood lies. Nevertheless, so strong is the power of the Holy Spirit that even the silence and secrecy of the brotherhood is finally being broken by a blessed few, and all because the moral and spiritual cost of not speaking out is far more devastating. A Second Pentecost is driving its most powerful and penetrating winds though some of the truly ordained Church Fathers as well. They are standing side by side with the priesthood of the people as those called by Christ to serve.

Included with the good holy fathers are the ordained men who left the priesthood to marry and whose priesthood is welcomed warmly by the priesthood of the people. These are the priests who left the privilege attached to priesthood and could not in good conscience profess celibacy and maintain a relationship in secret. Unlike the majority of their sexually active brothers in the priesthood, these are the ordained men who could no longer live that lie. Among the priestly men of conscience is the ex-Jesuit priest Charles J. O'Byrne, who presided at John Kennedy Jr.'s wedding and funeral and who left the priesthood recently because of how hypocritical it is about sex. A column in New York's *Daily News* reports him saying:

> Seminary life was hypocritical, but I tried to live with it and called it ambiguity. I became aware that there was

> sex all around me. For awhile I was angry. After all, I had enjoyed sex before I entered religious life and had determined to renounce it. Now people who have never had a sexual experience were having them—with the equivalent of churchly blessings. For me, the contradictions proved too much, and I decided to leave the active ministry.[4]

These priests remain among us, many of them still called to serve. Thousands of married and unmarried priests are part of the Second Pentecost, standing side by side with the priesthood of the people. Organized into groups such as Corpus and Rent-a-Priest, or unorganized but ministering wherever they are called to serve, the men who left the priesthood in good conscience can be found wherever and whenever priestly people come together. They, too, are part of the Second Pentecost, acclaimed and ordained by the priesthood of the people to help bring about the rebirth of Catholicism.

Most important among those joining the priesthood of the people are the faithful people themselves, Catholics in and out of the pew. It's ordinary Catholic families who have always held together Holy Mother Church, and it's those faithful ones who hold her together now. The new priesthood is all the people of the church who are rising up and demanding a full and truthful account of criminal abuses and who will never be silenced again. It's priestly people who are taking the Catholic Church to court in order to make them serve the same justice they command the rest of the world to serve. The signs of the times all point to the stirring resurrection of the priesthood of the people, people taking religion back into their own sacred hands and homes where it belongs, and where it was given to us in baptism. The greatest changes we've seen in this crisis have happened within the priesthood of the people, none of whom will be entrusting their souls, their children, or their money to the Catholic Church in the same way again. A rapidly growing number of Catholics, in and out of the pew, are blindly obedient no more. Catholics have changed more in the past few years than we have in the past two thousand. What else can that be but divine intervention? A Second Pentecost.

The heart and soul of religion lies far more in the community of believers than it does in its priesthood, and never has that been clearer. Christianity began with a handful of believers and that's all it takes to keep alive the Holy Spirit of Christ. Just two or three to gather together in that way does it. And there are far more Catholics than that coming together now in unprecedented ways, good sisters and priests among them, organizing locally and nationally, moving the church to change, preparing the way for its rebirth. We have every reason to believe that what we have seen and heard thus far of the crimes and sins of the fathers is only the tip of an iceberg as old and hardened as the church itself. And for as awful as it's going to get, these are the excruciatingly painful but blessed changes that have been dying to happen for centuries. The power of the Holy Spirit moving right now through the heart and soul of every Catholic could hardly be more forceful, and has all the makings of a Second Pentecost. Only this time, the priesthood of the people is much smarter, silent no more, and strengthened still by the sisterhood of women, just as it was in the beginning.

8

The Sisterhood of All Women

THE CALL TO SISTERHOOD is not a voice that only nuns hear. From what I see, the call to sisterhood lies secretly buried within the soul of all women, longing and waiting to be heard. What I find most enchanting about the call to sisterhood is how important, even holy, it regards a woman's need to get together with other women; and though most women do not seek to live sisterhood in religious life, getting together regularly with one another somehow answers that call. So sacred is such getting together among women that it becomes a heartfelt ritual for many of us, a mysterious rite of sisterhood to be nourished and protected for generations of women to come.

Years before I noticed the sisterhood of nuns, I loved my mother's monthly "Girls Night Out" with eleven other women who called themselves the Chères Amies, the Dear Friends. With the exception of December, when the Chères Amies had their Christmas get-together with husbands for an evening of dinner and dance, they always took turns meeting at one another's houses for a night of food, drink, and cards—usually pinochle or bunko. Prizes were valued at a whopping $3.00, $2.00, and $1.50. They paid monthly dues (with which they sometimes went out to lunch), picked the gardenia as the club flower, "Doodlee-Do" as the club song, and planned a big lakeside picnic each summer for the Chères Amies families.

I still remember my sisters and I sneaking as close as we could without being seen, straining to hear what they talked about at the monthly meetings that provoked such hearty laughter into the night. I remember that laughter more than anything else and still envy whatever it was that made those dear friends laugh so hard and so long, as though they held it in and waited all month to release it. Between club meetings these dear friends talked on the phone frequently, filling each other in on the details of their daily lives. And those who lived near one another—my mother, Shirley, and her best friend, Estelle Nowosinski—often got together for a cigarette-and-coffee talk after getting all their children off to school (each had five, three girls first, then two boys). They also called each other *dollka,* a Polish term of endearment between girlfriends, and referred to us as *little dollkas*. We were all dollkas then, and still are whenever we see one another.

Not only did the Chères Amies celebrate births, weddings, and successes of each other's family members, they also came to offer one another comfort, support, and meals-on-wheels in the event of sickness and death. Such was the sisterhood among the Chères Amies, and such was the friendship among these women that they became family in all the ways that matter most. Out of the Chères Amies mysteriously grew this whole other kind of family, drawn and held together by the lifeblood of sisterhood, the kind of sisterhood I imagined I'd find in religious life. And I did.

Three Chères Amies survive today, my mother (but not her best friend) among them. All three keep in touch and meet on occasion, though the monthly get-togethers are long gone. So divine and indestructible is the sisterly bond among these women that I cannot help but see their friendship as one of the earliest seeds of sisterhood sown in my soul. The first divine call I heard to sisterhood was that of my mother and her Chères Amies sisters. Every time I think of them, I'm reminded of an Emily Dickinson poem, "The Soul Selects Her Own Society." The Chères Amies were that kind of society.

Every woman I know tells similar stories of sisterhoods to which their mothers belonged, and every woman I know tells stories of similar groups to which they belong. They all speak of groups, large and small, which cultivate true loyalty and enduring bonds of love and support, as well as the best and most hilarious of times. In retrospect, I understand this call to sisterhood as a kind of primal instinct among women, a heartfelt call to friendship in which a level of divine comfort is found, as is the affinity of soul mates. Such "soul societies" always form out of some shared experience, at some turning point or difficult time in life. For example, the Chères Amies came together during World War Two, when part of each meeting was spent putting together packages and writing letters to their soldier husbands; an extraordinary source of sisterly support for women left alone during the war, most raising young children. My sister Debbie gets together with three other women monthly to play Scrabble. Calling themselves Scrabblettes, they came together originally because no one at home wanted to play with them. Like the Chères Amies, their children went to school together, and the Scrabblettes helped raise them all. As an honorary Scrabblette, who attends a few meetings a year, I can tell you that far more talking, eating, drinking, and laughing goes on than does finishing even one game of Scrabble. True soul food is served to our soul societies, and the Scrabblettes dish out the best.

Such are the ordinary mysterious ties that continue to bind women together in sisterhood, and such is the sisterhood by which I still love being bound. My life is full of sisterhoods and always has been. One of the most extraordinary was called The Secret Order of Judith—closet revolutionaries who saved the world over dinner and Manhattans. A table community of ten colleagues, the Judys consisted of eight women and two men (Judes). At least once a month we cooked up some enchanted evening, an evening of Judyism—a potluck gourmet meal, a cause to celebrate, a moon ritual, and the divine pleasure of one another's company. That was one powerful sisterhood that still is. The Secret Order of Judith is scattered over the country now, but the Judys keep in touch and so Judyism lives. Keeping in touch is a divine power in sisterhood, both in and out of religious life. The sisterhood of all women comes from the same divine call. The call to a sisterhood in which women are treated by one another as equal, and every woman's voice, life, and laughter is treasured as divine. No wonder the Catholic sisterhood regards as holy the need for women to get together with one another. Their lives become nourished in divine ways only sisters know.

A similar kind of sisterhood is emerging among women in the Catholic Church, with all the signs that look like a Second Pentecost. Nothing angers, wakens, and moves the soul of most women like the abuse of children, and even more profound is the awakening and enlightenment that happens when it's done by priests in the name of God. Even the most faithful and obedient Catholic women (good sisters included) are now counted among the church's faithful dissenters, many speaking their minds for the first time. Slowly but surely, one by one, Catholic women are waking to all the ways in which they have been used and abused by the priesthood. Bound by submission and subordination, but silent no more, a sisterhood is rising in the Catholic Church, the likes of which we've never seen. When we sleeping beauties awaken to the whole truth, that's when we'll see how quickly the mountains of clerical deceit can be moved. Women have always been the backbone and caretakers of Holy Mother Church, as well as the keepers of its silence. If women and their children stayed home one Sunday, the whole world would see how empty and nonexistent the Catholic Church is without them. That's how silently powerful the presence of women is in the church. That's also how powerful their faith is. There is no church without it.

We have not yet heard the voices of women who've been tormented by the church's teachings against them, nor have we heard from women who have been abused in relationships with priests, including a significant number of sisters. Wait until those women waken fully and begin to speak. When that day comes we will see how divinely powerful the sisterhood of women can be. When that day comes we'll also see how divinely powerful the priesthood of women can be. While we've just begun to understand the ways in which we've been victimized and betrayed by the Church Fathers, enlightenment will grow as the new priesthood and the new sisterhood waken fully, come together, and move forward. While our hearts may be troubled and afraid over all that's coming to light, we have God's word and promise that the Holy Spirit of truth will be with us in the hearts of the faithful. Catholics all over the world have been shaken and wakened soulfully by the sins of the fathers. A divine power so like that of a Second Pentecost is beginning to drive its wind and fire through the submissive and silent soul of Catholic women. The best of what women have to offer the Catholic Church is yet to come. When it comes to the divine power of sisterhood, in the church and in the world, we ain't seen nothin' yet.

What I see happening to women in the Catholic Church today is exactly what happens whenever women begin to hear and respond to their soul's call to sisterhood. Many women in the church are waking up to the experience of what it's like to be treated by one another as equals. When women begin to hear the call of one another to sisterhood, their soul wakens, enlightened and strengthened in ways the Church Fathers discourage. Acting because of and with friends is a powerful sustaining force. A sacred solidarity rises among women from their best friendships, enabling even the quietist women to break the silence and reveal the truth. By the divine power present in sisterhood, women become blessed with a mysterious strength and a Pentecostal energy that has all the feeling of wind beneath wings. Once women experience the divine power of sisterhood, we find we can no longer live without it.

What happens when women are called together in friendship, solidarity, and community is sisterhood's most powerful mystery. And there is no mystery more powerful in sisterhood than that which rises when women discover together the divine call to holy disobedience. Most who grew up Catholic did so believing that obedience and compliance with church authority was essentially good, right, and holy, while noncompliance or disobedience was clearly evil, wrong, and sinful. But now, after thousands of years of willing submission and unquestioning obedience, women in the church are shaken and wakened by the priestly abuse of children. Catholic women are both shaken and wakened to the soulful dilemma of what to do when the voice of God demands something different from the "divine authority" of the Catholic Church. When women begin to reconnect with the voice of God within their own lives and allow themselves to be moved by that Holy Spirit, they find that they can never become blindly obedient and soulfully submissive again, no matter how vehemently the Church Fathers exhort them to do so.

At least among the women I know (sisters included), the days of blind obedience are over, and for many women in the church they have been for quite some time. Just like Judith, Esther, and the other women liberators in the Bible, holy disobedience is revealed to women in the church as divinely motivated by a Holy Spirit who inspires faithfulness to one's conscience. One of the gifts of the Holy Spirit given to the church today is the divine gift of holy disobedience. Given that the infallible voices of church authority continue to fall from grace, we are called to pay close attention to our own divine voice and listen for what we hear revealed as true. When lies become the common language of the Church Fathers, we are called by the Holy Spirit to listen to our souls and the soulful voices of one another in order to hear truth revealed. Unquestioning obedience to church authority has lost its credibility, and the current crisis of faith in the Catholic priesthood leaves us with no other choice but to turn to one another in seeking the truth. Both in and out of the pew, women are finding one another and coming together in what looks like sisterhoods of the Second Pentecost, the holy disobedient likes of which Roman Catholicism has never known. Never again will women in the Catholic Church believe they are unworthy of priesthood.

In order to understand how disobedience can be holy, particularly for women forced by men (physically, spiritually, and emotionally) into submission and silence, it's important to look at the divine reasons for doing so. In exploring the questions of "why disobey," "when to disobey," and "which voices to disobey," we can see where the holiness in disobedience comes from. We can see how disobedience to church authority can become a holy path, a call of God we feel compelled to follow. Because Catholic women (still devoid of equality in the Catholic Church) have the least to lose in conscientiously objecting to the "divine authority" of Church Fathers, and have the most experience in being submissive, silent, and holy obedient, it's to the sisterhood of those women that we turn to for guidance in how to holy disobey. No one knows better than the women in the Catholic Church how holy and powerful disobedience can be. Those who've been beaten into submission for ages understand that perfectly.

The God who inspires holy disobedience within the women liberators of the Bible is the same true God who inspires holy disobedience within women in the Catholic Church today:

> The God of the humble,
> the Ally of the insignificant,
> the Champion of the weak,
> the Protector of the despairing,
> the Savior of those without hope. (Jdth. 9:11)

The divine reasons revealed by God for holy disobedience appear threefold: The situation is unbearable; the act of disobedience promises deliverance; and last but certainly not least, God is inexplicably still and silent, with divine intervention by a swift act of God not likely. In looking at what's happening in the Catholic Church, we are given every reason to holy disobey. Given what we know of the sins of the fathers, it's as though we are given a holy mandate to dissent with the grace of God. Holy disobedience emerges in the Catholic Church as a new law of God for the faithful. We no longer hear the voice of the priesthood as the infallible voice of God, and the divine mystique surrounding the privileged priesthood is gone. As we did in the beginning, we are once again discerning together the will of God revealed in the voice of the people, all the people, not just a privileged few.

Unbearable situations consistently inspire solidarity with all those oppressed by them, serving to motivate acts of defiance and disobedience. Whenever we find out that we've been lied to and betrayed, especially by religious authority, two responses are predictable: blind self-serving loyalty by some and confusion, dissent, and disobedience by others. While enforced silence may serve as an effective short-term method of damage control, it also provides a divinely fertile breeding ground for conflict and unrest, the intensity of which motivates us to do whatever we can to stop the madness. Unbearable situations, especially when created by "men of God," consistently work by the grace of the very same God to inspire acts of disobedience, as though the faithful have no choice but to protest in any way they can. Women in the church are beginning to feel that now. The safety and protection of children has moved the most obedient of women to see that these voices of "divine authority" must of necessity and by the grace of God be holy disobeyed.

Not only do unbearable situations inspire holy disobedience, but whenever the oppressive voice of "divine authority" claims to be above the liberating voice of God, holy disobedience is called for. Whenever "men of God" and their privileged, self-serving laws claim to be above the law of the land and the voice of its people, holy disobedience emerges as the law of God to follow. We are beginning to see that the voice of the Church Fathers is not that of the voice of God, and all claims to the contrary call for nothing but holy disobedience. With all the divine power of a Second Pentecost, even the most submissive and obedient of women in the church no longer support blindly and without question these "men of God" who hide the truth and betray the faithful in the name of God.

The "absence" and "silence" of God in the midst of the church's lies, crimes, and cover-ups provides the deepest motivation to risk individual or communal acts of defiance. When an act of God is not likely to undo clerical corruption, the faithful are left with no other alternative. In choosing disobedience, we do so trusting in the hidden workings of God while mindful at the same time that in the end our holy disobedient efforts may come to nothing. Just as Queen Esther prays before her defiant appearance before the king, so do we who contemplate holy disobedience pray:

> My Lord, our King, you alone are God. Help me who am alone and have no help but you, for I am taking my life in my hand. . . . Manifest yourself in the time of our distress and give me courage. . . . Put in my mouth persuasive words in the presence of the lion. . . . From the day I was brought here till now, your handmaid has had no joy except in you, O Lord. . . . O God, more powerful than all, hear the voice of those in despair. Save us from the power of the wicked, and deliver me from my fear. (Esther 4:12, 14, 23, 24, 29, 30)

In confronting what this priesthood has done to women and children, the silence and stillness (not absence) of God is all it takes to move women into a sisterhood bound by an unshakable faith in the God. As women begin to break the silences they keep, and rediscover within themselves the voice of God, they will never again obey blindly any authority but that of God, in themselves and in one another.

In trying to discern "when to disobey," it's becoming clear to women in the church, as it did to Esther, that disobedience presents itself as a survival technique and not an ordinary course of action. In other words, when the survival of Holy Mother Church is at stake, holy disobedience is the only course of action called for from the faithful. In doing whatever needs to be done to safeguard the sanctity of women and children in the Catholic Church, we meet those occasions when holy disobedience is the only course of action. The most important indicator of when to disobey rests within the divine ability of the Christian community to discern the right time and the most appropriate way, the "most educable moment," so to speak. The critical need to prepare oneself spiritually for acts of holy disobedience cannot be underestimated. Remaining in close prayerful contact with God is the condition that inspires all acts of holy disobedience.

The profound effects of communal discernment and solitary prayer in contemplating dissent appear to be twofold. In approaching every situation as an opportunity for divine intervention, our sensitivity is heightened, and we receive the strength and courage necessary to persevere. Holy disobedience serves as divine intervention when survival is at stake, when one has nothing to lose, and only after extended periods of personal and communal prayer. Recognizing the time and place to conscientiously object is a precarious task demanding the utmost care, prayer, and caution. Accustomed as women in the church have been to blind, holy obedience, we know what a precarious task holy disobedience can be. Women have a long history of being beaten to death for it. Women know that when their lives and the lives of their children are at stake, holy disobedience is the only divine alternative. The more women begin to see and understand what's been done to them in the name of God, the more they will come together to ensure that such abuse and oppression never happen to them or children again. In discerning "when to disobey," all women need to do is read the daily news to see that the divinely appointed time is now.

Every thinking Catholic knows instinctively by the grace of God which voices of "divine authority" warrant nothing but the most holy acts of disobedience. Three timeless voices of the Church Fathers can be heard as those authorities with whom no one should comply: voices that are abusive, demeaning, and deceptive; voices motivated by fear of widespread insubordination;

and voices that seek to silence and eliminate all that challenge their "divine authority." All three voices appear to be the only language Church Fathers know. And all three voices warrant nothing but the most holy acts of disobedience.

No one knows how abusive and demeaning the voice of the Catholic priesthood can be more than the women and children who have been diminished by their teachings. As the sisterhood of women in the church grows and strengthens, even the most silent and submissive will begin to demand that the Catholic Church treat them as equal (as sisters do), and treasure as divine their priestly lives and voices. Once the women of the church waken completely and see how profoundly these "men of God" have abused them and their children, they will never obey sexist voices again. In sisterhood, women grow to see that when they hear voices that demean and abuse them, what they also hear is the call of God to holy disobedience, to reject all abusive voices as evil regardless of who they come from. When the sisterhood of women grows and strengthens in the church and throughout the world, women will never again allow themselves or their children to be abused in any way.

Equally vocal in Catholicism, especially among the highest of church authorities, are those voices motivated by fear of widespread insubordination. To illustrate what these voices sound like, there is a scene in the Book of Esther where the king is at a banquet with his male cronies and commands Queen Vashti to appear before them naked with only the royal crown on her head. When she refuses outright to be humiliated like that (and most likely sexually abused), we are told that "the King's wrath flared up, and he burned with fury" (1:12). How dare she deny his kingly request? What follows is reflected in the thinking of Church Fathers today and could very well be the biblical foundation for the divine conspiracy to protect the male ego. In one single act of female insubordination, the queen not only offends the king, but every other man in the kingdom. Strange, but still true, one small but significant act of disobedience by the queen and the well-being of all mankind is undone completely.

> Queen Vashti has not wronged the King alone, but all the officials and the populace throughout the provinces. . . . For the Queen's conduct will become known to all the women and they will look with disdain upon their husbands when it is reported. . . . there will be endless disrespect and indolence. (Esther 1:16–19)

The profound disturbance of male authority by the solitary voice of one woman's disobedience remains just as baffling and revealing today. And the Church Fathers today, like biblical kings then, still seek outright to suppress and silence any voice of dissent out of fear of "endless disrespect and indolence." What a divine twist of fate we witness today in seeing how those priestly voices motivated by fear of widespread insubordination are met with nothing but the "endless disrespect and indolence" they inspire and deserve. Voices of "divine authority" that work to silence and eliminate those who challenge them call for nothing but holy disobedience.

In fearing the worldwide insubordination of women, the king issues an "irrevocable decree" so that "all women will henceforth bow to the authority of their husbands, ensuring that each man might be master in his own house" (1:20–22). The oppression and exploitation of women finds expression in the notion of "irrevocable decrees," infallible laws and teachings that cannot be changed no matter who they oppress. We can see that any law or teaching that seeks to oppress out of fear of "endless disrespect and indolence," or seeks to silence and eliminate all who challenge the "divine authority" of Church Fathers, is revealed in the Book of Esther as a divine invitation for creative acts of disobedience. As a matter of fact, divine activity peaks at the height of its power when such abusive voices are disobeyed. When the Gods appear still and silent, the holy disobedient voices of women appear to speak powerfully on their behalf.

As women in the Catholic Church (and in the world) become wakened fully to the divine call of sisterhood and the holy power of disobedience, then and only then can the mountains of clerical abuse and deception be leveled. What we experience now as a crisis of faith in the "divine authority" of Church Fathers signifies the exhausted end of something evil and oppressive, and the painfully slow beginning of something as universally liberating as that of a Second Pentecost, a new priesthood, a new sisterhood, and a rebirth of Catholicism the likes of which we haven't known in two thousand years.

9

The Rebirth of Catholicism

SO WHAT HAPPENS NEXT? Is this the end of the Catholic Church? Is this curtains for Catholicism? When we look at the response of the Church Fathers to the sex crimes and scandals that continue to surface and horrify the world, we have every indication that these "men of God" have no intention of revealing the whole truth. On the contrary, every effort is being made at the highest levels of church authority to ensure that the whole truth will never be revealed. Given the papal blessing of the Vatican, and superiors of men's religious congregations (like Jesuits, Benedictines, Franciscans, etc.) who insist on handling abuses internally, we find Church Fathers continuing to hide behind their canon laws, statutes of limitations, and the privileged privacy of incriminating documents. Regardless of what the new guidelines and papal apologies intend for us to believe, the lying and evasive actions of church leaders continue to speak much louder than any of their pious and repentant words.

The Church Fathers with the most to hide and the most privilege to lose are likely to consider then pursue the escape route of bankruptcy (moral, spiritual, and financial) as the only way out of the mess they created. Filing for Chapter 11 would suspend action in hundreds of civil suits and protect the most scandal-ridden archdioceses from new lawsuits being filed against them. Filing for bankruptcy also means that clerical accomplices would no longer to be subject to answering questions in pretrial depositions, or, like Phoenix Bishop Thomas O'Brien, would do so only if granted full immunity from prosecution. Escaping the truth is what we see. While spokespersons for the Archdiocese of Boston call reports of bankruptcy "speculative and premature," no thinking Catholic believes that for a moment. Already declaring morally and spiritually bankruptcy, filing for Chapter 11 appears to be a natural next step. Minimizing the scandals and doing everything in their priestly power to make it go away is all that matters to the Church Fathers. That's why we see nothing but matters getting worse.

In Springfield, Massachusetts, for example, the church still supports convicted pedophile priest Father Lavigne, a primary suspect in the murder of one of his victims. In a November 17, 2002, article in the *Springfield Union News,* staff writer Bill Zajac writes:

> Two former officers who helped investigate the 1972 slaying of a Springfield altar boy say Springfield Roman Catholic Diocese officials knew 30 years ago that a priest who was the prime suspect was believed to be a sexual abuser. . . .
>
> The retired officers' comments are in direct contrast to church officials' statements that they did not receive the first accusations of abuse against Lavigne until 1986.
>
> . . . The diocese has revealed 168 of the 699 pages in Lavigne's file. Diocesan lawyers claim the rest of the documents are protected by several privileges, including priest-penitent privilege.

Though convicted of sexual molestation charges in 1992, Lavigne received no jail time and ten years of probation. One can only wonder how many clerical aiders and abettors it took to orchestrate that deal. Protected by ordained privileges, the Church Fathers demonstrate no intention of telling the whole truth, not even when it involves murder. Not even the suspected murder of a child by one of its priests provokes the outrage of these "men of God." That's how entrenched and deeply rooted the Church Fathers are in criminal thinking. If murder fails to move them, then how can there be hope for priestly reform? Is this the end of the Catholic Church? To a priesthood of privilege and their criminal ways, millions of Catholics pray every day that it is, indeed, the end.

In Los Angeles, the daily news is no more hopeful. The Archdiocese of Los Angeles considered challenging a new law in California effective January 1, 2003, which lifts the statute of limitations on molestation cases in which the abuser is knowingly kept on the church's payroll. In a letter read to all parishioners throughout California, the bishops in California complained that because some of the allegations were so old it would be impossible to determine the truth. They also explain that their pastoral intent is to prepare the people for the financial drain on church resources that the new legislation would cause, so much so that they warn of even further cuts in educational and social services. This is the archdiocese that just built and dedicated a $190 million cathedral, with operating costs the archbishop estimates at $10,000 per day. Even so, the bishops portray themselves as not at all devoted to the accumulation of wealth, but simply the humble stewards of the financial assets that really belong to the people in the parishes. What nearly everyone but the bishops see is another shameless and calculated public relations effort by the archdiocese to gain public support for the church at the expense of the victims. In other words, absolutely nothing has changed in Los Angeles. Matters have only gotten worse.

In parishes and dioceses across the country, news continues to surface of the sexual misconduct of priests that goes unpunished despite the bishops most recent commitments to zero tolerance. In a November 30, 2002, article in the *Washington Post,* "Catholics Question Gray Areas of Abuse," staff writer Alan Cooperman reported that Bishop Frank Rodimer of Paterson, New Jersey, newly restored a suspended priest to active ministry after a review board (five lay Catholics and three priests) concluded unanimously that though the priest's behavior was "inappropriate," it did not meet the definition of *sex-abuse* adopted by the bishops and the Vatican.[1]

> The alleged victim told the board that the priest touched his genitals in bed at the priest's private home in the early 1970s, according to the victim's lawyer. . . . "Granted my client had his underwear on at the time, so the touching was on top of a thin layer of clothing," said the lawyer, "but it's incredible to me that they decided it was merely 'inappropriate.'"

What victims and nonvictims fear happening is indeed happening. The letter of the law has already killed its Spirit. Those priests who are onetime offenders or "simply" accused of lewd and lascivious conduct will be put back in ministry. Regardless of what deviant priests do, their priesthood remains untouched. Once a priest, always a priest.

Cooperman reported also of a Milwaukee priest repeatedly charged by police with indecent acts, "including a 1989 arrest for engaging in sexual activity with a 34-year-old truck driver and a 1999 charge of 'prostitution-masturbation' for which the priest paid a $1000 fine." In giving the priest a parish assignment (which parishioners protested), a spokesman for the archdiocese defended the church's action, noting that none of the charges involved a minor. "I'm not saying it doesn't matter. I'm just saying he's never been accused of sexual abuse by a minor, and the charter that was adopted in Dallas and modified in Washington only deals with minors." Hard to believe? Not anymore. The letter of the law has already killed any goodwill that may have been intended. Once again, all we see and hear, loud and clear, is that nothing has changed in the criminal thinking and privileged behavior of the Church Fathers and those who support them. The blind are still leading the blind.

From coast to coast it appears as though all we will continue to find with church leaders is nothing but a defiant refusal to admit the truth, much less reveal the truth. Nothing so far, not even the agony and death of victims, has moved the hardened hearts and empty souls of those "men of God" who have no regard for the sacredness of truth. When the law of the land and the dissenting voice of people fail to force Church Fathers to see the truth, it's not likely that anything will, not even their own self-destruction. Only criminal minds are that immune to the truth, and criminal minds are what we see protecting the Catholic Church's priesthood of privilege.

We can, however, even in these darkest days of Catholicism, take comfort in the voices of the faithful, liberal and conservative, which cannot and will not accept under any circumstances sexual depravity and promiscuity in its priesthood. We can also take comfort in the ancient wisdom of the *I Ching,* the Book of Changes, which reveals that all the evil these "men of God" continue to heap upon Holy Mother Church will only continue to undo them one hundredfold.

> Here the climax of darkening is reached. The dark power at first held so high a place that it could wound all who were on the side of good and light. But in the end it perishes of its own darkness, for evil must itself fall at the very moment when it has wholly overcome

> the good, and thus consumed the energy to which it owed its duration.[2]

Is this the end of Catholicism? We have good reason to believe that it is when every day now we see so many in its highest priesthood perishing from their own darkness. To ending the destruction of Holy Mother Church by its priesthood, the faithful pray every day, "Let it be." Let the kind of Catholicism created by these "men of God" end right now. While the priesthood of privilege at its highest levels of authority sees no problem with a clerical culture of sexual depravity and promiscuity, the priesthood of the people do, and they've seen enough.

The greatest comfort we can take lies in the most infallible truth of all: In the end always lies a new beginning. While the priesthood continues to serve its own undoing, something else is happening in the community of the faithful. For those who believe in resurrections, every ending holds the divine promise of a new beginning, and from what I see happening in the Catholic Church, this is one new beginning that has only just begun. What I see happening among Catholics, in and out of the pew, is nothing other than a new beginning—a new priesthood and sisterhood in the Catholic Church, the priesthood of the people and the sisterhood of all women. There already is a rebirth of Catholicism unlike anything we've seen since the first century. And now, just as in the beginning, the disciples are leading the way.

It's Catholics in and out of the pew, awakened so rudely, who are demanding a full and truthful account of all the priestly abuse, lies, and cover-ups. It's the priestly people (good nuns and priests included), who are the only true church Catholicism has left. And just like the Jesus Movement resurrected, the priesthood of the people are all Catholicism needs to return to its divine beginnings. All the signs of the time point to a growing resurrection of the priesthood among Catholics. And even though Church Fathers continue to ignore and silence the voice of the faithful, nothing can stop the rebirth of Catholicism fully under way. Catholics have changed more in the past year than they have in the past two thousand. The Church Fathers and their loyal supporters may not have changed, but millions of Catholics have. All over the world Catholics are rising from the dead silence they've kept for centuries and are wakened to their own priesthood. We are already witnessing a rebirth of Catholicism among millions of Catholics, another miraculous resurrection that's only just begun, but even in its beginning, the divine voices of the people can be heard loud and clear.

We Catholics are now hearing voices we've never heard before. Voices that have been silenced into submission for thousands of years are beginning to speak, and in doing so find that they will never keep that kind of deadly silence again. Voices of the faithful. Voices of victims. Voices of women. Voices of liberals and conservatives speaking for the first time as one. Voices of abused nuns breaking the silence. Millions of Catholic voices are being heard now, all of them revealing divine truths the Church Fathers can no longer condemn in silence. Even voices of the ordained are daring to speak. Priests brave enough to break the silence of their own priestly privilege are beginning to speak out, regardless of the personal cost.

A December 2, 2002, ABC news broadcast in Arlington, Virginia, reported the story of a "whistle-blower priest" punished by his diocese for telling the truth.[3] In exposing the sexual misconduct of several priests in three northern Virginia parishes, Fr. James R. Haley, the whistle-blower, is now facing unspecified charges that could lead to his defrocking. Arlington Bishop

Paul Loverde is seeking to punish Father Haley for testifying in a deposition about sexual misconduct and corruption in the Arlington diocese. Diocesan officials say that Father Haley violated a priestly order of silence that "was issued in order to avoid scandal, to maintain ecclesiastical discipline and to protect the reputation and privacy of both the faithful and priests of this diocese." Father Haley is currently on a "voluntary leave" according to the diocese, but a "forced leave of discernment" according to Haley himself. A national conservative Catholic group is rallying to his support, believing Father Haley should be rewarded for his actions rather than punished by Bishop Paul Loverde.

> "Father Haley is being punished for exposing corruption," said Stephen Brady, president of Roman Catholic Faithful. "It's clear that the church hierarchy in this country is in meltdown. A bishop can do practically anything and remain in good standing. Meanwhile a priest blows the whistle, and he's persecuted."[4]

Even so, we are beginning to see signs of holy disobedience in the priesthood. More ordained voices are breaking the silence they've been ordained to keep, regardless of the loss of priestly privilege. And standing firmly behind them are voices like the Roman Catholic faithful in Arlington, who will no longer tolerate the clerical corruption covered up and perpetuated by the bishops. The voices we are hearing today in the Catholic Church sound like the voices of Catholicism being reborn, a resurrection of the Catholic Church, the likes of which we have no idea.

What we are experiencing today in the Catholic Church is both a holy breakthrough and a divine turning point, a breaking through mountains and centuries of clerical deceit in order to return again to where we began. The voices we hear in Catholicism sound like those of the Jesus Movement, voices that do not seek to destroy one bit of the divine truth of Catholicism, only to fulfill its promise. There is no hatred for the Catholic Church in the dissenting voices I hear. Only a passionate love for Catholicism can be heard in those who hate its abuses, a love so divine that any compromise with evil in the church is not possible. Just as in the Jesus Movement, so, too, do the faithful believe that all crimes and misdemeanors in the priesthood must be openly discredited, brought out into the open, and banished forever.

A new form of Catholicism is beginning to emerge, though not in contradiction to its most sacred teachings and traditions. Quite the contrary. I see no attempt by anyone to dump the sacred truths of Catholicism along with its daily lies. All I see is an unprecedented effort by priestly people to bring back the original vision in a new way. The rebirth of Catholicism I see happening bears all the divine signs of a return to the loving ways and means of the Jesus Movement—to a discipleship of equals, to house churches, to table communities, to leaders who know how to serve, even to ordination (or resignation) by acclamation. Those changes are already happening in Catholicism, and they've only just begun.

In revealing how divine the painful parts of life can be, the *I Ching* reveals how unnecessary it to force or hasten any rebirth. By the grace of God and the power of the Holy Spirit (hidden not absent), everything comes of itself at the appointed time. "After a time of decay comes the turning point. The powerful light that has been banished returns. There is movement but it is not brought about by force. . . . The movement is natural, arising spontaneously. For this reason the transformation of the old becomes easy."[5] In being given sadness, confusion, anger, and frustration, the transformation that's already happening in the Catholic Church is so easy we hardly notice. In one of his "Letters to a Young Poet," Rilke writes about the sacred sadness that many Catholics know:

> You have had many sadnesses, large ones, which passed. And you say that even this passing was difficult and upsetting for you. But please, ask yourself whether these large sadnesses haven't gone right *through* you. Perhaps many things inside you have been transformed, perhaps somewhere, someplace deep within your being, you have undergone important changes when you were sad. . . .
>
> That is why the sadness passes: the new presence inside us, the presence that has been added, has entered our heart, has gone into our innermost chamber and is no longer even there,—is already in our bloodstream. And we don't know what it was. We could easily be made to believe that nothing happened, and yet we have changed, as a house that a guest has entered changes. We can't say who has come, perhaps we will never know, but many signs indicate that the future enters us in this way in order to be transformed in us, long before it happens. And that is necessary.[6]

That explains how the Catholic Church can be transformed and reborn without notice and without one stroke of the papal pen. Rilke explains how full our sadness is of divine intervention, of secret transformational forces at work. The sadness does not come to bind us or paralyze us; it comes to set us free. So much happens that never meets our eye. Behind the scenes, for example, theologians have been preparing the way for decades, returning to the beginning of Catholicism, returning to the Holy Spirit of truths revealed and not the literal way in which we interpret truth infallibly. In calling us back to the original vision of the early church, we already have a theology built on the Holy Spirit. We have sacred truths and traditions on which to build. And we have a new priesthood rising. The transformation of priesthood in the Catholic Church has begun and is well on its way to gathering the full strength of the Holy Spirit and the full power of a Second Pentecost.

All separatist tendencies are excluded from the new priesthood. With declining male vocations and a refusal to recognize the priesthood of women, a less-priest-centered church is inevitable by demographics alone, as is a less-nun-centered sisterhood. Given a quickly growing priesthood of the people dedicated to service, inclusiveness, and the infallibility of change, accompanied by a sisterhood no longer blindly obedient, the male-only priesthood has already been transformed. There are parishes all over the country in which a transformed priesthood and sisterhood have been serving the church for decades. In the September 3, 2002, issue of *The New Yorker,* Paul Wilkes tells the story of one such parish, and one priest's battle for a more open and inclusive church. Fr. Walter Cuenin, pastor of Our Lady Help of Christians in Newton, Massachusetts, had this to say about encouraging vocations to the priesthood:

> "This is going to sound a bit off the wall," he said, "but I'm going to ask you not to pray for vocations. But to pray that the Church will have the strength and the courage to acknowledge the vocations we already have. Exceptional women are waiting to serve. We have married men who would make wonderful priests. We don't

> need more vocations—they are already here. Let's just accept them."[7]

Father Cuenin also invited more than one hundred priests to his parish to discuss pastoral concerns about fund-raising for the Boston archdiocese while it is contemplating bankruptcy, and in the wake of newly released documents revealing priests abusing women and nuns (as well as children) and using drugs. The *Boston Globe* reported on December 5, 2002, that Cardinal Bernard Law barred all "archdiocesan-sponsored or archdiocesan-related meetings" from taking place in Father Cuenin's parish. According to *Globe* staff writer Michael Paulson, the cardinal's secretary, Rev. Arthur M. Coyle, sent an e-mail to the heads of archdiocesan agencies (but not to Cuenin) which read as follows:

> Good Morning, All! Because of some past issues, as well as current issues being addressed, the cardinal announced at a cabinet meeting this morning that until further notice no archdiocesan-sponsored or archdiocesan-related meetings, programs, workshops, etc. are to be held on the grounds of Our Lady Help of Christians in Newton.[8]

While no explanation was offered for this directive, it's clear that the cardinal is a master of issuing "irrevocable decrees" inspired by the mortal fear of widespread insubordination, one of those voices of "divine authority" that call for nothing but the exercise of personal and communal holy disobedience. It was those same priests who days later called for (and received) the resignation of Cardinal Law—an unprecedented move in the Catholic priesthood, resignation by acclamation.

When we look at parishes like that of Father Cuenin in Newton, and Father Scahill in East Longmeadow, where parishoners are withholding financial support of the Archdiocese of Boston, we see movements of a church already transformed. The transformation of the old priesthood of privilege has already happened at Our Lady Help of Christians and Saint Michaels, regardless of what Cardinal Law did and didn't do. Not even those at the epicenter of the sex scandals and crimes can stop the rebirth of Catholicism. With all the divine signs of a Second Pentecost, Father Cuenin's parish has grown by thousands when most parishes in this country have diminished by thousands. The transformation of the old is just that easy. All it took was one good father's acceptance of the priesthood of the people, with no thought of its cardinal consequences.

The rebirth of Catholicism I see happening will continue to happen with and without the Church Fathers. The true leaders and "men of God" emerging in the ordained priesthood are those priests who stand among us as those who come to serve. And those priests who work fearlessly to cultivate a discipleship of equals are the "men of God" Catholics are listening to and following. Even without any major change of church laws, the Christian community is returning to "ordination by acclamation," to recognizing as priest those "men of God" who are priestly because of the love and respect they inspire, and to whom position and power mean nothing. Privilege is no longer accepted by the people as part of priesthood.

The inertia, the indifference, and the self-interest that led to the decay of the old priesthood is being replaced by a new commitment to service and the power of a Holy Spirit that reveals that the ending of the corrupt priesthood of privilege will be followed by a glorious new beginning. The transformation of the old is just that easy, and it's taking place in the midst of the crimes and scandals. No church laws need to be changed. No new popes or bishops are necessary. The hearts and souls of Catholics are already changed by the power of a Holy Spirit like that of a Second Pentecost, making the transformation of the old so easy that it's done before we notice. And not over dead priests' bodies.

Among Catholics long gone or newly gone from parish churches, they, too, have discovered a rebirth of Catholicism. The emergence of house churches and table communities happened thousands of years ago for the early Christians and decades ago for many Catholics, as did an acceptance of the Gospels as their rule of life. In the Holy Spirit of the Jesus Movement, many Catholics exercise their priesthood in small Christian communities. Called upon to witness weddings, bless babies, anoint the sick and dying, and offer forgiveness, many of us are priests in the ways the Church Fathers proclaim infallibly that we can't be. While we may not be "real priests" in the eyes of the privileged priesthood, we are ordained so by God in baptism and by the people who call us to serve now. Outside of the Catholic Church there already is an active priesthood of Catholic women and men whose priestly service is ordained and accepted as sacramental by those they're asked to serve.

In and out of the pews are millions of Catholic parents struggling alone and together to raise children in a Christian family, with the Catholic prayers, traditions, and rituals they hold sacred. Out of necessity, there is a rebirth of Catholicism among parents who will not entrust their children to the Catholic Church now, maybe never again. Those parents who share similar views and concerns about Catholicism are also returning to the beginning, returning to the only law that matters according to Jesus Christ: teaching children to love one another and to not be mean. And never to stare because it makes people feel uncomfortable. Parents, too, are taking religion back into their hands, into their homes, and into their families, where religion began and belongs.

The rebirth of Catholicism I see happening outside parish life has all the divine signs of a Second Pentecost, including the rise of a world religion like that of the first Pentecost, a divine message that "every nation under heaven" can understand. In bringing back the original vision of Catholicism in a new form, the universal message of loving our enemies is one the whole world can understand as divine. While some dismembered Catholics move toward religions (like Episcopalian or Lutheran) more in keeping with their beliefs, most seem in search of a spirituality that treasures as sacred the truths we hold in common, and not those teachings that divide us and set us apart. If teachings divide and set us apart, I don't know how in God's name they can be true. Absence of hatred and privilege, and a commitment to nonviolence and equality, characterize the priestly people; a religion in which, for the second time in two thousand years, the mission is that "all may be one," that there be no such thing as enemies.

Holocaust victim Etty Hillesum writes about the kind of belief I find in small communities of Catholics, even among those who share the anger and disgust over the clerical corruption and deceit they find inside the church:

> The absence of hatred in no way implies the absence of moral indignation. . . . I know that those who hate have every reason to do so. But why should we always have to choose the cheapest and easiest way? It has been brought home forcibly to me here, how every atom of

> hatred added to the world makes it an even more inhospitable place. . . . It's not right for a human being to take the easy way out.[9]

In the Catholicism I see reborn, inside and outside of the Catholic Church, there is no hating, excluding, condemning, silencing, abusing, or killing anyone in the name of God. In and out of the pew, I hear Catholics speaking in languages everyone can understand and being understood by everyone who listens. The universal Christian language of love and understanding has that priestly power.

We have only just begun to see, both in and out of the church, what Catholicism will look like when Catholics return to the beginning and become moved to take religion back into their own priestly hands and homes. Our eyes have not seen and our ears have not heard the miraculous things that will happen when we listen to the voice of God speaking in one another and let ourselves be led by that Holy Spirit. "Just as the sun shines forth in redoubled beauty after the rain, or as a forest grows more freshly green from charred ruins after a fire, so too the new era appears all the more glorious with the misery of the old."[10] That's the rebirth I see happening in Catholicism, as one by one, the silence we've been bound to keep begins to speak. In one no longer silent voice, we're now coming together as Catholics in ways we never have. Regardless of what happens to the Catholic priesthood in the months and years to come, the sacred hope as Catholics, both in and out of the pew, lies in how well loved and cared for Holy Mother Church was, is, and always will be in the priestly hands of the People of God. We need not let our Catholic hearts be troubled or afraid no matter what comes to light in the future. After two thousand years of miraculous survival, we have every good reason to believe that all manner of things will be well.

AFTERWORD

ONE QUESTION REMAINS that begs to be asked. Because it tends to be a conversation stopper, I find it fitting to ask the ultimate question here: Has the time come for the American Catholic Church to be independent of Rome? Those who see all roads of clerical corruption leading to Rome ask seriously if that time is coming. And those who believe as the Sicilians do that "fish smells from the head down," also find the question begging. Given two thousand years of clerical resistance to reform is enough to make anyone wonder if we have any choice for church survival but to separate and be self-governing. As events continue to reveal the truth, it's likely that a growing number of Catholics will be asking that question. I did. In ending this book I found that question begging to be asked. Has the time come for the American Catholic Church to secede from the Roman Catholic Union?

All I can do in the end is ask the question because I have no idea what the answer is. The question alone is so far beyond where we are that the answer lies there as well. We are not at that point yet where we can understand the question or its answer. At least I'm not. Nor is anyone I asked. Some stared at me in stunned silence as though I had spoken heresy. I felt as if I were asking if someone should get divorced after two thousand years of Holy Matrimony. How dare I? In the minds of many, that will never happen. We Catholics survived the Dark Ages once, we'll do it again, and this time the Reformation will work.

Many believe that things will change and we will survive. And regardless of what happens, the American Catholic Church will never secede from the Roman Catholic Union. That is beyond question. End of book.

Even though I couldn't agree more, the question remains. As a Catholic woman, I also feel as though I'm asking if someone should seek a divorce after two thousand years of abuse. After ages of sexism and the refusal to change, what are the odds that the Church Fathers will reform now? They don't even admit to the problem. As a Catholic woman in the sisterhood, returning to the Jesus Movement of the early church looks mighty appealing. A discipleship of equals. Table communities. House churches. Leaders who serve. Believers in the divinity of women and children. I'm there already. Who wouldn't trade in religious abuse for such divine life? And in a country where democracy is treasured by law as sacred, what more fitting place and time than here and now to become a holy democratic Catholic Church? In witnessing the downfall of the priesthood, many find in the destruction a divine sign that the time has come to return to the Jesus Movement and begin again. That's the only saving grace for Holy Mother Church. The answer is to secede from union with Rome and return to the beginning. End of book.

Like the unprecedented changes already happening in the Catholic Church, this is another question we'll answer without knowing we've done it, and we will have been given the inner strength to accept it. That's already happening. We are being given the strength we need to get through these Dark Ages. We are being led through this dark night of our Catholic souls and guided in the rebirth. No one needs to know the answer, nor should we lend credence to those who say they have it. The answer will be given to all of us. The answer lies in the whole church and will come from the new priesthood, the new sisterhood, and the newly reborn Catholic Church. The best we can do right now is let it be. Some questions are best left in the lap of the gods, and this feels like one of them.

No matter how we look at it, the question remains, the kind of question gods ask. Seceding from any union is the holiest of decisions, and asking the question begs for divine intervention, especially after a holy union more than two thousand years old. We Catholics are in the midst of a powerful transformation, a divine intervention unlike any we've experienced. As the silences break and the truths reveal themselves, the answer will come. The answer always comes from the heart of the problem. If we revere as holy the questions we ask, we can be sure the answers given will be divine. And we can find evermore comfort, no less divine, in this heartfelt plea from the poet Rilke and me:

> I would like to beg you, as well as I can, to have patience with everything unresolved in your heart and try to love *the questions themselves* as if they were locked rooms or books written in a very foreign language. Don't search for the answers, which could not be given to you now, because you would not be able to live them. And the point is, to live everything. *Live* the questions now, perhaps then, someday far in the future, you will gradually without even noticing it, live your way into the answer.[1]

I couldn't agree more completely. Question answered. End of book. "Vitality begun." Blessed be.

NOTES

The following abbreviations are used in scriptural references for books of the Old and New Testaments:

Old Testament

Ezek.	Ezekiel
Gen.	Genesis
Jdth.	Judith

New Testament

Acts	Acts of the Apostles
1 Cor.	1 Corinthians
Gal.	Galatians
Matt.	Matthew
Rom.	Romans

Part One

Introduction

1. Bill Smith, "Nuns as Sexual Victims Get Little Notice," *Saint Louis Post Dispatch,* January 5, 2003, A1.
2. Mary Nevens Peterson, "Nun Sex-Abuse Report Does Not Surprise Sisters," *Telegraph Herald* (Dubuque, Iowa), January 18, 2003, A1.
3. Garry Wills, *Papal Sin: Structures of Deceit,* New York: Doubleday, 2000, p. 186.
4. Elizabeth Abbott, *A History of Celibacy,* New York: Scribner's, 2000, p. 110.
5. Ibid., p. 103.

1. Priesthood in the Beginning

1. Elisabeth Schussler Fiorenza, *In Memory of Her,* New York: Crossroad, 1992, p. 176.
2. Elizabeth Abbott, *A History of Celibacy,* New York: Scribner's, 2000, p. 318.
3. Garry Wills, *Papal Sin: Structures of Deceit,* New York: Doubleday, 2000, p. 156.
4. Ibid., p. 155.
5. *Women & Christian Origins,* edited by Ross Shepard Kraemer and Mary Rose D'Angelo, "Reconstructing 'Real' Women from Gospel Literature:

The Case of Mary Magdalene," by Mary Rose D'Angelo. New York: Oxford University Press, 1999, p. 105.

2. Priesthood in the Middle Ages

1. Elizabeth Abbott, *A History of Celibacy,* New York: Scribner's, 2000, p. 101.
2. Jo Ann Kay McNamara, *Sisters in Arms: Catholic Nuns through Two Millennia,* Cambridge, Mass.: Harvard University Press, 1996, p. 238.
3. E. R. Chamberlain, *The Bad Popes,* New York: Dorset Press, 1986, p. 43.
4. Ibid., p. 60.
5. Evelyn Underhill, *Mysticism,* New York: Dutton, 1961, p. 70.
6. *The Complete Works of Saint Teresa of Jesus,* volume II, translated by E. Allison Peers. "Interior Castle," p. 187; "Conceptions of the Love of God," p. 357.

3. Priesthood Now

1. Richard Johnson, Page Six: "Just Asking," *New York Post,* May 16, 2002, p. 10.
2. A. W. Richard Sipe, *A Secret World: Sexuality and the Search for Celibacy,* New York: Brunner-Routledge, 1990.
3. Laurie Goodstein, "Trail of Pain in Church Crisis Leads to Every Diocese," *New York Times,* January 12, 2003, pp. A20–21.
4. Arthur Jones, "Discontent and Disaffection Grow as L.A. Archdiocese Dismantles Ministries," *National Catholic Reporter,* October 11, 2002, p. 6.
5. Ibid.

Part Two

Introduction

1. Jo Ann Kay McNamara, *Sisters in Arms: Catholic Nuns through Two Millennia,* Cambridge, Mass.: Harvard University Press, 1996, p. 357.

4. Sisterhood in the Beginning

1. Jo Ann Kay McNamara, *Sisters in Arms: Catholic Nuns through Two Millennia,* Cambridge, Mass.: Harvard University Press, 1996, p. 2.
2. Elizabeth Abbott, *A History of Celibacy,* New York: Scribner's, 2000, p. 39.

5. Sisterhood in the Middle Ages

1. Jo Ann Kay McNamara, *Sisters in Arms: Catholic Nuns through Two Millennia,* Cambridge, Mass.: Harvard University Press, 1996, p. 311.
2. Ibid., p. 193.
3. Elizabeth Abbott, *A History of Celibacy,* New York: Scribner's, 2002, pp. 142–143.
4. Ibid., p. 143.
5. McNamara, p. 357.
6. Ibid., p. 317.
7. *Beguine Spirituality,* edited by Fiona Bowie, translated by Oliver Davies (Spiritual Classics Series), New York: Crossroad, 1990, pp. 11–12.
8. Ibid., p. 17.
9. Ibid., p. 35.

10. *Julian of Norwich: Showings,* translated by Edmund College and James Walsh, New York: Paulist Press, 1978.
11. Marguerite Porete, *A Mirror for Simple Souls,* translated by Charles Crawford (Spiritual Classics Series), New York, Crossroad, 1990.
12. Ibid., p. 147.

6. Sisterhood Now

1. Jo Ann Kay McNamara, *Sisters in Arms: Catholic Nuns through Two Millennia,* Cambridge, Mass.: Harvard University Press, 1996, p. 626.
2. Ibid., p. 636.
3. Translation: "The Congregation of Holy Cross" and "Mother of Sorrows, pray for us."
4. *Constitutions of the Congregation of the Sisters of the Holy Cross,* Notre Dame, Ind.: Ave Maria Press, 1962, pp. 6–7.
5. *The Complete Works of Saint Teresa of Jesus,* volume I, translated by E. Allison Peers. "The Life of the Holy Mother Teresa of Jesus," pp. 1–300.
6. *Lesbian Nuns: Breaking Silence,* edited by Rosemary Curb and Nancy Manahan, Tallahassee, Fla.: The Naiad Press, 1985.
7. Ibid., p. 14.
8. Ibid., p. 238.
9. Ibid., p. 188–189.
10. Ibid., p. 312.
11. Sarah Lydall, "Irish Recall Sad Homes for 'Fallen' Women," *New York Times,* November 28, 2002, p. A3.
12. Elizabeth Abbott, *A History of Celibacy,* New York: Scribner's, 2000, p. 389.

7. The Priesthood of the People

1. Garry Wills, *Papal Sin: Structures of Deceit,* New York: Doubleday, 2000, p. 264.
2. Ibid., p. 239.
3. Thomas P. Doyle, "Conscientious Objections: Priest Calls on Brethren to Do the Right Thing," *Boston Herald,* November 17, 2002, p. 23.
4. *New York Daily News,* August 20, 2002, pp. 20–21.

9. The Rebirth of Catholicism

1. Alan Cooperman, "Catholics Question Gray Areas of Abuse," *Washington Post,* November 30, 2002, p. A2.
2. *I Ching: Or, Book of Changes,* translated by Richard Wilhelm, Princeton, N.J.: Princeton University Press, 1981, p. 142.
3. "Whistle-Blower Priest in Trouble with Diocese," *ABC 7 News,* December 2, 2002.
4. "Whistle-Blower Priest in Trouble with Diocese," *ABC 7 News* online, December 2, 2002.
5. *I Ching,* p. 97.
6. Rainer Maria Rilke, *Letters to a Young Poet,* New York: Vintage Books, 1986, pp. 82–85.
7. Paul Wilkes, "The Reformer: A Priest's Battle for a More Open Church," *The New Yorker,* September 2, 2002, p. 104.

8. Michael Paulson, "Curb Imposed on Newton Parish," *The Boston Globe*, December 5, 2002, p. A1.
9. Etty Hillesum, *Letters from Westerbork*, New York: Pantheon Books, 1996, pp. 36, 37.
10. *I Ching*, p. 257.

Afterword

1. Rainer Maria Rilke, *Letters to a Young Poet*, New York: Vintage Books, 1986, pp. 34–35.

INDEX

ABOUT THE AUTHOR

KAROL JACKOWSKI, a nun since 1964, lives in New York City, where she is a member of the Sisters for Christian Community. She is the bestselling author of *Ten Fun Things to Do Before You Die* and *Sister Karol's Book of Spells and Blessings*.